# PRAISE FOR *THE PREVAILING CHURCH: CONFRONTING THE FIVE GIANTS OF CULTURE*

‿o‿

"The body of Christ so desperately needs to learn how to influence society in such a way that people are drawn to us. We have the answers to the world's problems, but have been fumbling our God-given assignment. It is not time for us to cower in the corner of adversity; it is time for us to shine! This is our greatest moment. That's why I'm eager for you to read Dr. John Jackson's new book, *The Prevailing Church*. His compelling words will remind you that Jesus created us to be the salt and light of the world, to transform the culture around us and change the world!

John Jackson is a father in the Lord who relentlessly pursues the kingdom and exudes wisdom and grace. He simply and practically breaks down keys and concepts that will embolden you to become a catalyst to bring the kingdom and cultural transformation wherever you go. As Dr. Jackson puts it, "Our world is desperately in need of the light and life of the gospel. We have the opportunity to demonstrate that light and life by the way we love and live engaged in culture, not isolated from it." I couldn't agree more and am thankful for this timely and crucial book. I highly recommend it."

> — KRIS VALLOTTON
> LEADER, BETHEL CHURCH, REDDING, CA
> CO-FOUNDER OF BETHEL SCHOOL OF SUPERNATURAL
> MINISTRY, AUTHOR OF THIRTEEN BOOKS, INCLUDING
> *THE SUPERNATURAL WAYS OF ROYALTY*,
> *HEAVY RAIN*, AND *SPIRITUAL INTELLIGENCE*

"My friend and colleague, Dr. John Jackson, is sounding a clarion call at a most opportune time in history for the people of God, the Ekklesia. His call for the Church in America to live engaged in culture and not isolated from it is compelling and leads us to cons... the question, "H... we then live?" that he answers so brilliantly... Goliath. Given Dr. Jackson's credentials as

with his lifelong experience as a leader and pastor to pastors, it is no surprise that *The Prevailing Church* is a scholarly work, but also extremely practical and inspirational as you live your life for Kingdom impact that will lead to the transformation of cities and nations, and ultimately, the fulfillment of the Great Commission. Definitely this a must-read book!"

— Dr. Ed Silvoso
Founder, Transform Our World
Author, *Ekklesia: Rediscovering God's Instrument for Global Transformation*

"John Jackson issues a powerful call to spiritual awakening and revival. We have everything we need to become the church we're meant to be, but to get there, we'll need to let go of much of what we're holding onto. Jackson gives us concise, practical steps to become the church we all long for. This is a gift to the body of Christ for today."

— Margaret Feinberg
Author of *More Power To You*

"It's no secret that 2020 was a year of revelation and apocalypse, meaning a year in which hard truths were uncovered and exposed worldwide—especially here in America. One of these truths is that the church has fallen into serious spiritual sickness, so much so that it's almost unrecognizable from what Christ first called us to be. Instead of shying away from this truth, *The Prevailing Church* does the hard work of facing it head-on in order to heal and restore who we were always meant to be. What's more, it offers us readers ways to face these truths so that we might repent and throw down the giants of our own cultural creation. *The Prevailing Church* is a welcome and necessary message of hope, truth, and transparency for these times and a light at the end of the tunnel."

— Albert Tate
Co-founder, lead pastor, Fellowship Church, Monrovia, CA

"Churches are going through a time of sifting—as Peter and the disciples had been during Jesus' arrest and crucifixion. Sifting is all about the faith—what the faith is, who the faith is in, and how the faith is applied. And we are learning all over again about true authentic Christian faith. Thanks to John Jackson, *The Prevailing Church* points Christians in the right direction in understanding authentic Christianity. Read with a soft heart and an open mind."

— ED STETZER
WHEATON COLLEGE

"What the world needs most, Chuck Colson used to say, is for the church to *be* the church. This book not only clarifies what that looks like, but also deftly describes five key things currently crippling our witness and influence. In it all, we are given a way forward, a vision for what could be. May it be so."

— JOHN STONESTREET
PRESIDENT, THE COLSON CENTER

"I've known Dr. John Jackson for over twenty-five years and seldom have I met anyone more committed to the ministry and vision of the local church. John is a local church maniac in all the best ways. His latest book is a bold call to Jesus followers to re-examine, rethink, and renew the kind of impact that is possible through local churches of Jesus Christ all over the globe. Prepare to be stretched and dream big."

— GENE APPEL
SENIOR PASTOR, EASTSIDE CHRISTIAN CHURCH
ANAHEIM, CA

"This book is past due for the church and our call to help shape culture. Dr. Jackson offers clear, compelling, and practical advice on how the church is to be the transformational force it can be. The chapter on the five giants that shape culture could stand alone as a book worth purchasing. Read this today, but only if you're ready to be called to a challenge from Jesus."

— WILLIAM VANDERBLOEMEN
FOUNDER AND CEO VANDERBLOEMEN SEARCH GROUP

"In *The Prevailing Church*, John Jackson champions the idea that the people of God should be actively engaged in the world to make it possible for people to experience life as God intends (the Kingdom). His call for the church to come out of hiding and demonstrate the kingdom is a welcome and compelling message. The stones you carry in your own bag may or may not match John's, but his assertion that we are called to be viral kingdom agents should make us assess what we can do to reclaim what hell has stolen."

— REGGIE MCNEAL
AUTHOR OF *KINGDOM COME* AND *KINGDOM COLLABORATORS*

"I have been a fan of John Jackson for many years now. His intensity for the Church to be all she was meant to be inspires me to no end, particularly in these difficult days. If this vision is to happen, we have some big giants to face. John calls them out without holding back and tells us how to slay them. I have my slingshot in hand and five smooth stones ready for battle. I pray for you to join the cause."

— RANDY FRAZEE
PASTOR AND AUTHOR OF *HIS MIGHTY STRENGTH*

"With the passion of a God-fearing and willing prophet, Dr. John Jackson speaks the mind of God to the church of God. This is a heartfelt cry and wake up call to the church. *The Prevailing Church* is a clear and concise revelation of where the church is and where the church should be. John calls us to awake out of sleep and run and meet our giants head on. Thanks John, for being the friend of God and for being our friend by telling us the truth."

— BISHOP VAUGHN MCLAUGHLIN
FOUNDING & SENIOR PASTOR,
THE POTTER'S HOUSE INTERNATIONAL MINISTRIES
CEO KINGDOM PLAZA MALL

"John Jackson has brought together his years of experience as a Christian leader and his thoughtful and insightful understanding of both Scripture and culture to call the church to renewed faithfulness. *The Prevailing Church* offers a visionary exhortation, along with insightful guidance for followers of Jesus Christ in their personal witness and cultural engagement. I am happy to recommend this readable book, and trust that it will receive a wide circulation among various sectors of the Christian community."

— DAVID S. DOCKERY
PRESIDENT, INTERNATIONAL ALLIANCE
FOR CHRISTIAN EDUCATION

"John Jackson is a lover of the family, the church, and the world. *The Prevailing Church* is a call for the church to recover its mission in the world and make disciples of Jesus. Transformation is at the heart of the Gospel, and John hits at the heart with this book."

— DR. JIM GARLOW
CEO WELL VERSED

"God has always intended for the church to bring His kingdom from heaven to earth. I'm thankful for Dr. Jackson's unswerving devotion to the body of Christ and for writing this important manifesto. May a pure and powerful church emerge from the ruins."

— BRADY BOYD
PASTOR, NEW LIFE CHURCH,
AUTHOR OF *EXTRAVAGANT*

"President Jackson has written a cry of the heart to stir the faith community to action. As a pastor and educational leader, he boldly calls out our errors while also loving God's church. This book is from one of God's shepherds to encourage and help His sheep."

— JOHN MARK N. REYNOLDS,
PRESIDENT, THE SAINT CONSTANTINE SCHOOL

"The church was never meant to be the prey of culture. God designed the church to be the aggressor. Dr. Jackson does a great job of calling the church from retreating to advancing. It's time to kill the giant!"

— PASTOR GREG FAIRRINGTON
FOUNDING & SENIOR PASTOR,
DESTINY CHURCH, ROCKLIN, CA

"This is a must-read book for the times we are in, seemingly, as the church is in retreat. The enemy is working hard to erode the impact of the church in the world today. He's using current events to bring fear, division, and every other evil work, but it's time for us to *rise up* for the kingdom of God to be salt and light in the world! This is a defining moment for the church, and Dr. Jackson's book will empower you to stand up and step out in the authority God has given you. I declare, as you read this book, that it will cause you to be more bold, more courageous, and more compassionate about making a difference in our culture today."

— Dr. Phillip Goudeaux
PASTOR OF CALVARY CHRISTIAN CENTER

"My friend and brilliant cultural observer, Dr. John Jackson, has packed into this little book how our culture can be lifted out of its death spiral. He tells us that it is not too late, but it will take some clear-eyed examination of our individual and corporate behavior. His prescription is for churches in every county in the United States to become prevailing churches, rather than pandering social clubs. His words are strong but accurate prescriptions for the church to embrace its fivefold ministry. If the church is going to be salt and light in our current day, the truths of Dr. Jackson's analysis must reach the church and its leaders. He calls the church to speak out and make positive changes on the five death-injecting elements in our society. "

— Dr. Gil Stieglitz
DISCIPLESHIP PASTOR, BAYSIDE CHURCH, GRANITE BAY, CA
AUTHOR OF *BUILDING A RIDICULOUSLY GREAT MARRIAGE*
AND *WISE PARENTING*

· OTHER WORKS BY JOHN JACKSON ·

*The Right Choice: Choosing a College and Why it Matters*

*30 Days to Healthier Relationships*

*Finding Your Place in God's Plan*

*God-Size Your Church*

*Leveraging Your Communication Style*

*Leveraging Your Leadership Style*

*Pastorpreneur*

*High Impact Church Planting*

# THE PREVAILING CHURCH:

Confronting the Five Giants of Culture

JOHN J. JACKSON, PH.D.

Jessup **Press**

*THE PREVAILING CHURCH:*
*CONFRONTING THE FIVE GIANTS OF CULTURE*

Published by Jessup University Press, 2121 University Avenue, Rocklin, CA 95765.
For more information about this book and the author, visit www.drjohnjackson.com.

**Copyedited by**: Jennifer Edwards, jedwardsediting.net
**Cover Design by**: Tanner Di Bella
**Book Design & Typography by**: Linné Garrett, 829Design.com

ISBN: 978-0-9884306-9-3 (print)
ISBN: 978-0-9884306-4-8 (e-book)

*Printed in the United States of America*

✣

*This book is dedicated to local church pastors and leaders*

*who love, lead, and live in dynamic relationship*

*to their fellowships and communities so that*

*the name of Jesus may be lifted up.*

*Thank you for longing to see the kingdom of God*

*manifested in your neighborhoods.*

# · CONTENTS ·

# · FOREWORD ·

I think many of us in America can agree that 2020 was one of the
most difficult years we have ever lived through.

The COVID-19 pandemic, social unrest, and divisive politics
turned our country upside down and in the process brought to the
fore some serious wounds — both individual and collective — that
are in desperate need of healing.

We realized how spiritually sick the American church is today,
and how it has been for many years.

We were forced to reckon with our giants.

In order to slay our giants, we must recognize where the church
in America went wrong and repent. Then, we must understand how
God intends his daughters and sons to shape culture.

That's why Dr. John Jackson's words in *The Prevailing Church:
Confronting the Five Giants of Culture* are vitally important. He
outlines five cultural giants we face:

*The giant of historical revisionism*
*The giant of abortion and euthanasia*
*The giant of religious repression*
*The giant of racism and injustice*
*The giant of identity and family*

Each of these giants deserves to be knocked down with a
"stone" of faith, as the shepherd boy David felled the giant Goliath

with one stone, believing God could do the impossible when his circumstances seemed to say otherwise (1 Samuel 17).

With a wisdom rooted in a deep understanding of Scripture and a warmth rooted in his love for people, John discusses how to renew and revive the church in America, that it might truly seek justice, love mercy, and walk humbly with God, so that His kingdom will come and His will be done, on earth as it is in heaven (Micah 6:8; Matthew 6:10).

If you desire to see the church in America restored, and if you are ready to face your giants, then read on.

> Rev. Samuel Rodriguez
> Lead Pastor, New Season Church
> President, NHCLC
> Author of *From Survive to Thrive:*
> *Live a Holy, Healed, Healthy, Happy,*
> *Humble, Hungry, and Honoring Life*

# · ACKNOWLEDGMENTS ·

I want to thank William Jessup University, our Board of Trustees, the wonderful teams that I am honored to serve with, and the amazing churches we partner with to **educate transformational leaders for the glory of God.**

I want to thank Destiny Christian Church and Pastors Greg and Kathy Fairrington for their friendship and leadership in our region and in our lives. I want to thank Kris Vallotton for his friendship and prophetic insights; Kris saw much of this "reset" in advance. I want to thank Ed Silvoso for his vision of the "ekklesia" and his passion for personal and cultural transformation in the power of the Holy Spirit. I want to thank Sam Rodriguez for his partnership in the gospel and his friendship in life.

I want to thank my precious children and grandchildren for the joy of being part of your lives...what a blast it is! Finally, I want to thank my precious wife, Pam, who is almost always ahead of me in hearing what the Lord is saying, and graciously standing beside me as we navigate the terrain of the present and future. Over four decades of life together means that I love you more today than yesterday but not as much as tomorrow.

# · INTRODUCTION ·

The year 2020 was full of multiple pandemics. Many aspects of the health, racial justice, media censorship, economic, political, and social pandemics had been brewing for years, but 2020 unleashed unparalleled pressures beyond anything experienced in the past many decades. At the beginning of Covid-19, I believed we would see this process: Reveal–Reset–Reentry–Revival/Reformation. As the Covid-19 journey has extended over the months, I have said that I was right on the words and wrong on the depth and duration. Part of the urgency in my spirit to write this book has been the breadth and depth of what has been revealed about our culture and the spiritual condition of our nation.

The events of late 2020 and early 2021 in our nation, including the violence at the capitol in early January, reveal some of the breadth and depth of our public division and anger. The wounds of our nation run deep and the healing required is likely to be generational. But my burden for the spiritual realities of our world (as described in Ephesians 6) proceeds and originates from the burden I have for the spiritual condition of the church in America. What we are facing in the nation and what we have become as the church in America are connected in the spirit and the flesh.

Let me be clear right here at the beginning. I am a lover of the family and a lover of the church. I believe the family was the first institution that God established in the earliest days of creation. The family is the foundation of society and culture. I also believe that God established His people in believing assemblies (what the New Testament calls "ekklesia"). I believe in the people of God, assembled together in communities of faith for worship, teaching, fellowship, ministry, and evangelism. I am for the fivefold ministry of apostles, prophets, pastors, teachers, and evangelists. I am for the equipping of the saints for the work of ministry. I am for the church being released in the world to be "salt and light" for the glory of Jesus. I am for the people of God fulfilling the prayer of Jesus that we might see "thy kingdom come, thy will be done, on earth as it is in heaven" (Matthew 6:10).

I've had the privilege to personally participate in, lead, teach, love, consult, and rejoice in the growth of megachurches across the country. Much great life and ministry has taken place in those settings, and I am grateful for the Jesus-honoring fruit that has been born. I am "for" any church that magnifies the name of Jesus. But I think virtually all discerning leaders will say that regardless of church growth and size, we are *not* seeing "heaven on earth" here in the United States (and for the most part, around the world). That discernment should cause us great concern and a burden for the spiritual condition of our present hour. I am burdened that many people in our modern churches, churches that I pastored as well, do not have a saving relationship with Jesus Christ. Second Peter 1:10 (NIV) tells us what we must do:

> "Therefore, my brothers and sisters, make every
> effort to confirm your calling and election. For
> if you do these things, you will never stumble."

Following Peter's confession of Jesus' identity in Matthew 16:18, Jesus declares that confession as the "rock" upon which He would build His church. Jesus then promises that the "gates of hell will not prevail against it." How is it that the "prevailing church" Jesus promised has been reduced to a convenience, consumer, and casual variation of Christianity? The word "prevailing" includes the meanings of "predominant, generally current, or having superior power or influence."[1] In no case would most observers describe the status of the Christian church in America using the word "prevailing." This Christianity we are generally experiencing here in the US, whatever else it is, is not producing biblical fruit and biblical witness in our families, our communities, or our nation. While those statements may seem judgmental, I firmly assert that they are fully biblical as we have a responsibility to judge the household of faith (1 Corinthians 5:12). We can know the root by examining the fruit, and the fruit of modern-day Christianity in America is not pleasing to the Lord. The giant of culture is immobilizing and neutralizing the witness of the church.

Now more than I recall ever occurring in my lifetime of almost six decades, I believe God is calling the church to *wake up, rise up,* and *stir up* the callings of God in our culture. We are called to *wake up* and see the destructive forces that have been unleashed in our midst. We are called to *rise up* and strengthen our hearts and hands for the work that is before us. We are called to *stir up* the gifts of the Spirit within us and walk in the power of the resurrection, declaring the kindness of God and calling our community and culture to repentance and humility before the person and work of Jesus Christ (Romans 2:4, 8:9–11). I believe God is calling forth a generation of spirit-filled and spirit-empowered followers of Jesus to live and walk in heavenly ambassadorships where they extend the kingdom of heaven on earth.

I am further convinced that the church must engage with the giants of culture. I know the prevailing church of Jesus Christ will indeed defeat the giants of culture. David, the simple shepherd boy, observed the giant Goliath shouting taunts against the army of God (see 1 Samuel 17). David determined to face Goliath on behalf of the people of God and was offended at the cowardice of the army of Israel. While initially resistant, King Saul finally consented to David being their representative and tried to outfit him with his own armor. David ultimately rejected Saul's armor and went out to face the giant with the power of his testimony of previous miracles God had performed.

David took his trusty slingshot and found five smooth stones. Facing the taunts and strength and weaponry of Goliath, David went boldly against him in the power of the name of God and defeated Goliath with a mortal blow. The armies of God conquered that day, and the name of the Lord was lifted in praise and glory that reverberates to our day. All because a shepherd boy refused to let the name of God be reviled and cower in fear before a giant. Five smooth stones defeated a giant of an enemy.

The church in America has been retreating against the giants of culture for many decades. In the pages that follow, you will learn the following keys to our future and receive understanding about our history. We will answer these questions:

- Why has the church in America retreated from cultural influence?

- Is there a biblical mandate for cultural transformation?

- How do the people of God live as "salt and light" in our world?

- What are the "five cultural giants" we must face in our present-day battle?

- How can we mobilize the people of God for kingdom impact?

I am believing for a prevailing church. As a pastor friend (Greg Fairrington) has said, "the easiest place for Satan to hide from a Holy God is in a dead church." I say "no" to the plan of the enemy to paralyze and fracture the bride of Christ and make churches dead. On the authority of the words of Jesus and in the power of His resurrection, I am declaring that the era of a passive, weak, disengaged, fear-filled church is *over*. The people of God are waking up, rising up, and stirred up for battle against the enemy. Though he is indeed a thief (John 10:10) and roars about like a lion (1 Peter 5:8), we declare that the only lion who matters is the Lion of the tribe of Judah, and Jesus is His name (Isaiah 11:6, Revelation 5).

Join me as we press in to hear the Spirit's call to the prevailing church that is emerging like a shepherd boy from the crowd...

# one

# THE CHURCH IN
# RETREAT

T he bride of Christ was never meant to be a retiring and reticent creature of comfort. Instead, the church is to prevail and push back the realms of darkness that have been exercising dominion over this rebellious planet since the moment of the fall in the garden. Some have been acculturated to a variation of the "watchmaker theory" that believes God "wound up" the universe and has set the course of actions to come; human freewill has little to do with affecting the course of events on the planet. But the clear and compelling story of Scripture is that God partners with individuals and groups of people gathered as the church (or "ekklesia") to accomplish His kingdom purposes on earth.

The return of Jesus to planet Earth, first as a babe in the manger, and second as a conquering king, is the greatest rescue story ever told. Jesus came to save, heal, and deliver from darkness and oppression those who have been captured by the enemy of their souls.

The fundamental mission of the church is to live to the praise and glory of God (Ephesians 1) by being ambassadors of reconciliation in the world (2 Corinthians 5) and discipling nations (Matthew 28) through the equipping of the saints by the fivefold ministry leaders—apostles, prophets, evangelists, pastors, teachers (Ephesians 4).

Instead of being an activist church, many in church life have defaulted to what has also been called the "blueprint" or "watchmaker" view as described above and have little to no engagement in society. We have often satisfied ourselves with our gatherings of insiders and have seemingly little to no passion for reaching those outside the household of faith. How has this worldview and behavior affected our nation?

Here are just a few modern assessments of the spiritual condition of our nation and of the church:

> 85 percent of young outsiders conclude that present-day Christianity is hypocritical. Half of young churchgoers agreed that Christianity is hypocritical.[1]

> Overall, 30 percent of born-again Christians admitted to at least one type of sexually inappropriate behavior in the past thirty days, including online pornography, viewing sexually explicit magazines or movies or having sex outside of marriage, compared with 35 percent of other Americans.[2]

> Among young outsiders, 84 percent say they personally know at least one committed Christian. Yet just 15 percent thought the lifestyles of those Christ-followers were significantly different from the norm.[3]

> Barna's 2008 survey found that only 9 percent of the general audience surveyed had a biblical

worldview, and those who claimed to be born-again Christians were 19 percent.[4]

In virtually every study we conduct, representing thousands of interviews every year, born-again Christians fail to display much attitudinal or behavioral evidence of transformed lives. For instance, based on a study released in 2007, we found that most of the lifestyle activities of born-again Christians were statistically equivalent to those of non-born. When asked to identify their activities over the last thirty days, born-again believers were just as likely to bet or gamble, to visit a pornographic website, to take something that did not belong to them, to consult a medium or psychic, to physically fight or abuse someone, to have consumed enough alcohol to be considered legally drunk, to have used an illegal, nonprescription drug, to have said something to someone that was not true, to have gotten back at someone for something he or she did, and to have said mean things behind another person's back. No difference.[5]

Here's a short history of Christianity attributed to Priscilla Shirer:

In first century in Palestine, Christianity was a community of believers.

Then it moved to Greece and became a philosophy.

Then it moved to Rome and became an institution.

Then it moved to Europe and became a culture.

Then it moved to America and became a business.[6]

And finally, from across the Atlantic comes this observation from Os Guinness:

> The problem with Christians in America is not that Christians aren't where they should be; the problem is that they're not what they should be right where they are.[7]

How then, did the church in America arrive at such a place? How did the national conscience seemingly change from a broadly (and admittedly flawed and failing) Judeo-Christian values-based worldview to a secular and systemically disengaged church absent from the public square and society without a defining moral compass?

In addition to the "watchmaker/blueprint" worldview, I believe that the church in North America has been the victim of two belief systems that have corrupted our engagement with society. The first diversion has been our acceptance of the "sacred/secular" divide. In this worldview, we have accepted the notion that human existence is divided into spheres. The sphere of church and religious activity and devotion is "sacred" and everything else is "secular." This view has allowed many in the church to pursue religious affection (or at least religious activity) divorced from cultural engagement. Sadly, we have then abandoned entire generations to a culture dominated by varying forms of hedonism, humanism, and secularism ensconced in cultural streams without a vibrant kingdom of God presence and witness.

Years ago, I was struck by pastor Terry Crist in his book *Learning the Language of Babylon: Changing the World by Engaging the Culture*, when I read these words,

> Several years ago, in a time of intense soul-searching, the Lord asked me this startling question: Who gave you the right to bargain off my property?

Though it was a simple question, it produced a major paradigm shift in my thinking. In a moment of revelation, I felt I understood the purpose behind the question. Like many others, I had sat down at that table of unilateral disarmament with the enemy and said to him, in effect, "Don't bother us and we won't bother you! You can have the kingdoms of this world – entertainment, the arts, media, politics, athletics, law, economics – and we will take our Sunday school programs, Bible clubs, Christian conferences and home Bible studies. If you leave us alone, we'll leave you alone."[8]

Not only did Crist share his personal revelation moment about the consequences of his "sacred/secular" mindset, he also began to do some digging in history where he discovered that even outside his tradition (Crist is a pastor in the charismatic stream), there was a strong worldview in the reformed tradition that confronted this destructive and bifurcated worldview. Crist discovered Abraham Kuyper, a leading and seminal voice in history from over one hundred years earlier. In his inaugural address at the Free University on October 20, 1880, Kuyper challenged the withdrawal of the church from the public sector by declaring,

"There is not one square inch in the whole domain of our human existence over which Christ, who is Sovereign over all, does not cry: 'Mine!'" This lecture formed the basis for Kuyper's teaching on "sphere sovereignty," when he divided "sovereignty in the individual social spheres" into seven basic areas – state government, family, religion, business vocation, education, science and the arts.[9]

I believe the "sacred/secular" divide to be a particularly toxic worldview. In my opinion, it has prevented the "priesthood of all believers" from taking place, as it has allowed pastors to be in charge of the "sacred" and for those not in "full-time" pastoral ministry to consider their vocation as "secular." Part of what I want to argue in the pages to come is that God is calling for a Second Reformation where we actually live out the Great Commission and disciple nations in every sphere of society. I believe the discipling, equipping, and releasing of the people of God to kingdom ministry across culture will be the foundational activity in the Second Reformation and that we are on the edge of that reformation even now.

The second deficient worldview is our eschatology, which is often "upstream" of our ecclesiology. In the turn of the twentieth century (1900), views of an extreme millennialism began to increasingly push Christians to believe that culture was the fallen incarnation and revelation of a world heading towards a cataclysmic end. The church was both powerless to change the trajectory and, in fact, the trajectory was the fulfillment of a prophetic order. While I have many friends in the premillennial camp and personally have no certainty at all regarding the exact timing and details of the return of Jesus Christ to the planet, I have become increasingly concerned about the effects of our eschatology on our ecclesiology. For some others, even those who do not accept and align with a premillennial view, they have believed that the social and cultural wars are already lost and that Christians should retreat to varied forms of isolation and rebuilding society in small clustered contexts (e.g., Rod Dreher. As an aside, I have deep appreciation for Dreher's work in *The Benedict Option* and *Live Not By Lies*. My argument is not with the content of his works but in their application by readers). In my view, any view of future events that causes followers of Christ to disengage from the world is missing the fundamental heart of God as Redeemer.

For me, it is critical that the church engages with the culture, no matter what your view of end-times events and chronology. We need to recognize the reason God left us here on the planet is to testify to His goodness, His grace, and to live to the praise of His glory. God is a redeemer and we who love Him are compelled to testify of His love and live and work redemptively for the sake of the planet. The cultural mandate to bring about "heaven on earth" is both a response to Jesus' own prayer and a present participation in His work. And while I agree that proclaiming the gospel of salvation for eternal salvation is our first responsibility, I do not believe it is our last. I am aware that this is not universally accepted in the church. Dave Hunt is another advocate against Christian activism and his viewpoint is represented here:

> "Christian activism" is not Christian. It represents a detour from the straight path the church is to walk before the world. It can confuse the real issues, lead to compromise and unholy alliances, and divert time and effort that would better be used in proclaiming the gospel. Weigh the demands upon your time and set priorities. Be fully engaged in rescuing souls for eternity.[10]

I agree that we must proclaim the gospel of forgiveness, but I believe the gospel of forgiveness is only a partial gospel. *The gospel of Jesus Christ is a gospel of forgiveness, healing, and deliverance.* When Jesus prayed that the will of God would be done "on earth as it is in heaven," He was making a proclamation of both intent and assignment. We who carry the life of the Risen One, empowered by the same Spirit that raised Jesus from the dead, have the assignment, authority, and power to manifest and extend the kingdom of God in every domain we encounter. Os Hillman, a powerful advocate for this worldview, has come to speak at William Jessup University (www.jessup.edu), where I serve as President. Listen to his encouragement here:

Making disciples of entire people groups and
nations is the end game. It is thrilling to consider
that the cry "Thy kingdom come. Thy will be done
on earth, as it is in heaven" makes heaven available
through you right now to potentially fix whatever
is broken in any earthly system you are assigned to.
This is God's desire. In the end the leaves of the
tree of life are "for the healing of nations."[11]

As we close this chapter, I want to share a powerful encouragement that I received a number of years ago about what cultural
transformation can look like. It has perhaps become too easy, due
in part to our worldviews, to see cultural decay as a natural result of
the end times or the unstoppable decadence of our times. I say *no*
to that future! We are called to be agents of transformation, and the
church is called to prevail against the darkness of our times. Read
these words and be encouraged! In the next chapter, we will start
to unpack more fully what Scripture says to us about our mandate
in the here and now.

James Hunter, in a 2002 Trinity Forum briefing,
highlights what sociologist Randall Collins says
about civilizations in his book *The Sociology of Phi-
losophies.* According to Collins, civilizations have
been defined by a very small percentage of cultural
philosophers who influence seven gates and sup-
porting networks since our birth as a civilization.
Hunter summarizes, "Even if we add the minor
figures in all of the networks, in all of the civilizations, the total is only 2,700. In sum, between 10
and 3,000 people (a tiny fraction of the roughly
23 billion people living between 600 B.C. and
A.D. 1900) framed the major contours of all world

civilizations. Clearly, the transformations here were top-down. What an amazing piece of information. Imagine that. Culture has been defined since the beginning of time by no more than three thousand change agents, a tiny fraction of the population."[12]

It doesn't matter if the majority of the culture is made up of Christians. It only matters who has the greatest influence over that cultural mountain. And the mountain of family must undergird all other cultural mountains.[13]

James Hunter, in his book *To Change the World,* states, "Imagine...a genuine 'third great awakening' occurring in America, where half of the population is converted to a deep Christian faith. Unless this awakening extended to envelop the cultural gate-keepers, it would have little effect on the character of the symbols that are produced and prevail in public and private culture. And, without a fundamental restructuring of the institutions of culture formation and transmission in our society—the market, government-sponsored cultured institutions, education at all levels, advertising, entertainment, publishing, and the news media, not to mention church—revival would have a negligible long-term effect on the reconstitution of the culture."[14]

"When the righteous are in authority, the people rejoice; But when a wicked man rules, the people groan."

PROVERBS 29:2 [15]

*two*

———

# THE BIBLICAL
# MANDATE FOR
# CULTURAL
# TRANSFORMATION

*I find it strange that "apathy" is clean, while
involvement is "dirty." Rather than dirty our
hands in the process of governing, we choose to allow
abortion, pornography, unabated perversion, and
moral deterioration to drown our communities and
eventually our families. Now that's dirty!* [1]

While I'd love to live in a God-honoring and Jesus-loving
culture, I recognize the gap between my desires and my
reality is often very real (just look at my waistline or my golf
score some day!). But far beyond my desire is the question of
what Scripture and the Spirit say to us. Is there a biblical mandate
for followers of Jesus to be involved in cultural transformation?
Or, as Hunt (see quote from previous chapter) and others have
argued, is cultural engagement really a distraction from the work

of proclaiming the gospel? Is the end-times trajectory of the planet so established under the sovereignty of God that we literally go against the will of God when we work towards incarnating the kingdom here on earth? These are weighty questions and I can only frame up a basic response here in this book. If you would like to delve further into this topic, I have provided a number of resources at the end of this chapter that provide robust arguments for why the church should be actively engaged in social transformation. I invite you to investigate them for yourself.

At this time, I'd like to provide a simpler and more nuanced outline to inform our next steps. For me, the compulsion to live out my faith in relationship with the world and mobilize the people of God for kingdom impact comes from my understanding of the heart of God in Scripture as it correlates with the present voice of the Spirit in calling His children to reach the world. In short, I believe the Scripture compels us to lift up the name of Jesus in word (proclamation) and deed (demonstration) for the purpose of offering redemption to a lost and broken world.

Here are some principles from the pages of Scripture that compel me:

1. **God is holy:** "Consecrate yourselves and be holy, because I am the LORD your God. Keep my decrees and follow them. I am the LORD, who makes you holy." (Leviticus 20:7–8)

2. **God invites us to know Him:** "Now this is eternal life: that they know you, the only true God, and Jesus Christ, whom you have sent." (John 17:3)

3. **Knowing God transforms us:** "For the grace of God has appeared that offers salvation to all people. It teaches us to say 'No' to ungodliness and worldly

passions, and to live self-controlled, upright and godly lives in this present age, while we wait for the blessed hope—the appearing of the glory of our great God and Savior, Jesus Christ, who gave himself for us to redeem us from all wickedness and to purify for himself a people that are his very own, eager to do what is good." (Titus 2:11–14)

So at a foundational level, the people of God are people of transformation. We who have come to know Jesus have experienced His grace, goodness, forgiveness, and love, and that encounter has transformed our lives. One might imagine, having experienced that transformation, Jesus would simply rescue us up to heaven! In my childhood, the TV show "Star Trek" was a big deal. They had a "transporter" that would "beam" our bodies to another place in an instance. Captain Kirk would often say to Scotty, "beam me up!" Surely if God wanted us to have an encounter and be transformed, He could then "beam us up" and get us out of here. However, Jesus actually prayed for something quite different:

I am coming to you now, but I say these things while I am still in the world, so that they may have the full measure of my joy within them. I have given them your word and the world has hated them, for they are not of the world any more than I am of the world. My prayer is not that you take them out of the world but that you protect them from the evil one. They are not of the world, even as I am not of it. Sanctify them by the truth; your word is truth. As you sent me into the world, I have sent them into the world. For them I sanctify myself, that they too may be truly sanctified. (John 17:13–19)

Two more principles are embedded in this passage:

4.  **This world is not our home, and Jesus did not pray for our removal from the world.**

5.  **Jesus prayed for our protection from evil through the truth of His Word.** This was a consistent theme for the apostle John. (See also 1 John 2:15–16, 5:3–5.)

Finally, Scripture repeatedly tells us that we are to live in such a way that world around us comes to know Jesus, the Savior. Colossians 4:5–6 tells us our conversations ought to be full of grace, and Matthew 5:14–16 tells us that we are to live in such a way that the world sees our good deeds and praises our Father in heaven. On the basis of these and many other passages, my sixth biblical principle is this:

6.  **We remain on earth to live as kingdom ambassadors and bring all whom we can to be reconciled to the Savior.**

    All this is from God, who reconciled us to himself through Christ and gave us the ministry of reconciliation: that God was reconciling the world to himself in Christ, not counting people's sins against them. And he has committed to us the message of reconciliation. We are therefore Christ's ambassadors, as though God were making his appeal through us. We implore you on Christ's behalf: Be reconciled to God. (2 Corinthians 5:18–20)

Ours is a complex time, so how should we live? Obviously, we need the strength of each generation to understand what the men of Issachar did in their time—they "understood the times and knew what Israel should do," (1 Chronicles 12:32). I believe the New Testament is replete with examples of kingdom ambassadorship principles that undergird this transformational mandate. For our purposes, let me simply highlight two of them.

Matthew 25 has a series of stories about the end of the age and how people have responded to the Master. The first two parables are about preparation (ten virgins and oil for their lamps) and accountability and stewardship (servants and the talents entrusted to them). The third parable has a compelling story of "sheep and goat" nations where Jesus describes separating people based on their responses to the thirsty, hungry, and imprisoned. Many who read these words are confused and immediately reject any implication that could feel like "works righteousness," or a pathway for earning one's salvation. I am in complete agreement that our salvation is not only completely free, but it is the unearned and undeserved gift of God. But I see no conflict here or elsewhere in Scripture. We are saved *from* death, destruction, and despair, *and* we are saved *to* life, hope, and abundance. Ephesians 2:8–10 captures what I think is the essence of the New Testament grace and works reality:

> For it is by grace you have been saved, through faith—and this is not from yourselves, it is the gift of God—not by works, so that no one can boast. For we are God's handiwork, created in Christ Jesus to do good works, which God prepared in advance for us to do. (Ephesians 2:8–10)

We are saved in a supernatural experience of grace, and the supernatural byproducts of this salvation are natural expressions of love and compassion that bring about the transformation of fallen creation back to alignment with our Creator. When Jesus' prayer includes the plea that it should be "on earth as it is in heaven," He is describing the coming of the kingdom of Heaven on earth in the person and lives of His people, empowered by the same Spirit that raised Him from the dead (see Romans 8:11).

The story of the church's birth in Acts 2 is perhaps more well remembered than the teaching and prophetic pictures in Matthew 25. What we know is that in Acts 2, there were signs, wonders, and miracles taking place as the power of the Risen Christ and the manifest presence of God were being demonstrated through the power of the Holy Spirit. This was a church meeting that became a historic touchpoint for generations of believers, up to our present day. We can only imagine the dynamic excitement of the new and early church as the miracles and wonders took place. But it is reasonable to ask, "What was the response of the surrounding communities?" How did the first-century community react to the formation of the church?

Acts 2:47 tells us that they were "enjoying favor with all the people. And the Lord added to their number daily those who were being saved." I think the template here is worthy of us grabbing hold of for today. A church that is experiencing the presence of God and His movement will see a harvest of new salvations and life in Christ as well as having favor in the community for their impact. The Matthew 5 exhortation to be "salt and light" in the world is for the purpose of having people give praise to God (we will explore this passage in depth in the next chapter). The spiritual condition of our modern-church reality can reasonably be evaluated by asking how many people give praise to God for what they see in church and in followers of Christ? I am burdened that the church often has little favor and little impact in our communities; the contrast with the New Testament church is stark.

Os Guinness has a couple of challenging things to say for our present discussion:

> In short, we must foster a robust discipleship with a faith worthy of our Lord—with a reach as high as the awe and majesty of God, as deep as the depths of the Scriptures, as rich as the stories and lessons of history, and as wide as the infinite varieties of the worldwide church. Unquestionably, culture creation requires time and perseverance. It is not a matter of harvesting mushrooms but of growing oak trees.
>
> The truth is, the power of God through his Spirit is always the all-decisive factor, and faith rests confidently in that final fact. But such is the character and the cultural shape of Christian truth that the practice of that truth carries enormous power too. In other words, when followers of Jesus live out the gospel in the world, as we are called to do, we become an incarnation of the truth of the gospel and an expression of the character and shape of its truth. It is this living-in-truth that proves culturally powerful. It is therefore entirely legitimate to inquire into how Christian faithfulness and obedience to the truth serve the purposes and the power of God to change the world.
>
> In short, the decisive power is always God's, through his Word and Spirit. But on her side the church contributes three distinct human factors to the equation: engagement, discernment and

refusal. First, the church is called to engage and to stay engaged, to be faithful and obedient in that it puts aside all other preferences of its own and engages purposefully with the world as its Lord commands. Second, the church is called to discern, to exercise its spiritual and cultural discernment of the best and worst of the world of its day, in order to see clearly where it is to be "in" and where it is to be "not of" that world. And third, the church is called to refuse, a grand refusal to conform to or comply with anything and everything in the world that is against the way of Jesus and his kingdom.[2]

Guinness provides a helpful (if stinging!) challenge for our churches as we understand what is happening within our churches and in our church relationship with the culture. It is my hope that the church, in all its many manifestations, will be found faithful in this generation. As such, my prayer also is that the body of Christ will be more intentional and proactive to make disciples and to reach and impact the communities around them.

God is calling His people to be agents of reconciliation, offering grace and redemption to the world around us. In our next chapter, we will begin to unpack what it means to live as "salt and light" in our often dark and drifting world. The person and work of Jesus, the clear and unequivocal teaching of Scripture, and the compelling work of the Holy Spirit in seeking for lost people to be reconciled to the Father is what animates us in this hour.

FOUNDATIONAL RESOURCES:

Donald Atkinson & Charles Roesel, *Meeting Needs, Sharing Christ*
Ray Bakke, *A Theology As Big As the City*
Matthew Barnett, *The Church That Never Sleeps*
William Bennett, *The De-Valuing of America*
Daniel Bernard, *City Impact*
Allan Bloom, *The Closing of the American Mind*
Robert H. Bork, *Slouching Towards Gomorrah*
Tony Campolo, *Revolution and Renewal*
Robert D. Carle and Louis B. Decaro Jr., *Signs of Hope in the City*
Stephen Carter, *The Culture of Disbelief*
Chuck Colson, *How Now Shall We Live?*
Chuck Colson, *Kingdoms in Conflict*
Jack Dennison, *City Reaching:*
    *On the Road to Community Transformation*
Dave Donaldson and Stanley Carlson-Thies,
    *A Revolution of Compassion*
Colonel Doner, *The Samaritan Strategy*
Barbara J. Elliott, *Street Saints*
Michael O. Emerson and Christian Smith, *Divided by Faith*
Wayne Grudem, *Politics According to the Bible*
Timothy J. Keller, *Ministries of Mercy: The Call of the Jericho Road*
Robert Lewis, *The Church of Irresistible Influence*
Robert Linthicum, *Scriptures Revealing God's Transforming Power*
Gabe Lyons, *The Next Christians:*
    *The Good News About the End of Christian America*
Erwin Raphael McManus, *An Unstoppable Force*
Sider, Olson, Unruh, *Churches That Make a Difference*
John Perkins, *Beyond Charity*
Robert D. Putnam, *Better Together: Restoring the*
    *American Community*

Rick Rusaw and Eric Swanson, *The Externally Focused Church*
Francis Schaeffer, *How Should We Then Live?*
Amy Sherman, *Restorers of Hope*
Steve Sjogren, *101 Ways to Reach Your Community*
Steve Sjogren, *Conspiracy of Kindness*
Eric Swanson resources (https://ericjswanson.com/wp-content/
uploads/2008/08/ten-paradigm-shifts.pdf)
Tom White, *City-Wide Prayer Movements*

*(Note: This is a partial list only and not a list of all Christian authors.)*

*three*

---

# LIVING AS SALT AND LIGHT IN THE WORLD

*Now it shall come to pass in the latter days*
*That the mountain of the LORD'S house*
*Shall be established on the top of the mountains,*
*And shall be exalted above the hills;*
*And all nations shall flow to it.*
*Many people shall come and say,*
*"Come and let us go up to the mountain of the*
*LORD, To the house of the God of Jacob;*
*He will teach us His ways,*
*And we shall walk in His paths."*

— ISAIAH 2:2–3 NKJV

I believe in and bleed for the local church in all its manifestations. I believe the passage from Isaiah 2 is a declaration that the church's best days lie ahead and that it is the will of God for it to be primary in His kingdom agenda for planet earth. The church (or "ekklesia") takes many forms across the planet, but wherever and however the assembly of believers gather, and wherever in the community it scatters, it is a visible representation of the invisible

Christ, manifesting His love and life to a world desperately in need of its witness. (See my friend Ed Silvoso's book *Ekklesia* in the bibliography for more descriptions of the biblical ekklesia movement in its modern context.)

It has been my privilege to serve as a local church pastor, denominational leader, church planter, author, leadership consultant, speaker, and university president. In all those roles, there is nothing that compares (in my view) with being able to see someone come to know Jesus Christ as Savior and then be rooted and grounded in their faith so that they become a reproducing disciple (see Colossians 2:6–7). Several years ago (in the late 90s), a member of my church was distraught about the condition of society and the church in America, and wrote asking me what we should do. My response was as follows, a preview of what would many years later become this book:

> I believe there is a basic ethic that informs our role as God-honoring people who are first citizens of heaven, and secondly citizens of this nation. The following is an outline of what I think individual people can do to be salt and light and righteous in a dark and darkening world. As I outline these ideas, I am reminded of the fact that Christ-followers around the world live in horribly difficult circumstances where they experience pain, depravation, and loss of life for following Jesus...and their faith is strengthened, not weakened. I believe, therefore, that our faith is not dependent upon America being a "Christian nation." If America becomes a decadent wasteland, Jesus is still the same "yesterday and today." The reason I believe that Christians should fight for righteousness in

our land is not to secure the truth of Christianity, but to provide for a righteous environment in which the Gospel of Christ can be taught and that our nation will be a light to the nations. I believe that Chuck Colson's book, *How Now Shall We Live?* is an excellent resource to be read along with Francis Schaeffer's seminal work, *How Should We Then Live?* Both of these works are supplements to a biblical foundation of citizen responsibility. To that end, I suggest the following as an outline of an ethic for US Christians:

1. Men and women committing their lives to Jesus Christ.

2. Men and women fulfilling their responsibilities as citizens: they vote, they support candidates with biblical/theological roots and voting records that are consistent with their biblical understanding and they engage their neighbors and friends in constructive conversation.

3. Believers gathering together in groups within churches and discovering ways to stand for salt and light on key issues. Clarity on what is biblical versus what is cultural (for example... support for the Contras during the Reagan years...what is clearly biblical versus what is an extension of a biblical truth?). These key folks are "arrowheads."

4. Churches taking a clear stand on clear biblical issues as per above. Different biblical leaders

have different areas of focus. I have a strong personal focus on the following four issues: Constitutional Law (I support Patrick Henry College and their focus on "original intent"), abortion (I believe it contributes to a culture of death and the devaluing of human life), pornography (I believe it demeans women, appeals to the base instincts of men, and leads to child exploitation), and homosexuality (I believe it is a progressive and subversive political and social agenda that is perhaps the most sophisticated of the above movements).

So, twenty-plus years later, why I am including my pastoral response to someone in a book I am writing now? Has my answer "aged" well? Or do I wish I would have written something different? Well, as you may have guessed, I think the answer gets it fairly right. Some of the language and focus may have been able to be sharpened...but I think I steered the person in an essentially correct fashion.

In my view, the fundamental mission of the church is to make disciple-making disciples of Jesus Christ. Part of being a disciple-making church community is a vibrant witness to the world (as we discussed in the last chapter) and learning how to do that in the particular cultural setting in which God has placed that community of believers. In a US context, I will often say to churches and people that "your address is not an accident; it is an assignment." I think this kingdom perspective equips us to live with discerning eyes and seek to understand what God is saying to us and asking from us as we are faithful to His redemptive mission in our world. So, as Francis Schaeffer asked and answered in the 1970s, "How should we then live" in light of the gift and heart of God, the biblical mandates we have reviewed, and the current cultural realities?

The first place I would like to start is to recognize that my experience with the Lord is absolutely key if I want to be part of a revival work of God. If I have not had a genuine personal encounter with the Lord, I have very little lasting value to offer the world around me. *You cannot give what you do not have.* Second, we need to recognize that we are not the first people to ever feel like we are swimming "upstream." Christians in the first centuries after Jesus were faced with culture and communities where the moral compass was broken. One only need to think about Rome, Ephesus, and Corinth in the first few hundred years after Christ; those communities make Las Vegas, San Francisco, and New York all look mild relative to sin and distractions. The writers of the New Testament spoke into those settings and equipped those first followers. I think they speak powerfully to us today as well.

Since we are not the first, we can keep learning from the clear instructions of the New Testament. As an example, Corinth was a place of rampant sexuality, worship of idols, a center of commerce, and a thriving metropolis. Church in that setting had some amazing and powerful things happening, and Paul was clear what a Jesus-centered faith was all about:

> Now, brothers and sisters, I want to remind you of the gospel I preached to you, which you received and on which you have taken your stand. By this gospel you are saved, if you hold firmly to the word I preached to you. Otherwise, you have believed in vain. For what I received I passed on to you as of first importance: that Christ died for our sins according to the Scriptures, that he was buried, that he was raised on the third day according to the Scriptures, and that he appeared to Cephas, and then to the Twelve. After that, he appeared to more than five hundred of the brothers and sisters

at the same time, most of whom are still living, though some have fallen asleep. Then he appeared to James, then to all the apostles, and last of all he appeared to me also, as to one abnormally born. (1 Corinthians 15:1–8)

A Jesus-centered faith ensures that we lay a foundation of the atoning death of Christ, His burial, and resurrection. Sadly, we operate in a world where the truth about Jesus and the authority of Scripture has been greatly diminished. In a previous generation, G.K. Chesterton warned, "The trouble when people stop believing in God is not that they thereafter believe in nothing, it is that they thereafter believe in anything." Part of our witness in the world is to be truthful, simple, and clear about what the Bible teaches about Jesus. Below is what I teach when I am offered the opportunity to do so.

## A Biblical View of Jesus

Jesus is **God incarnate** (God come to earth in the flesh).
- John 1:14

Jesus is God's **perfect substitute** sin offering.
- 1 John 3:5
- 1 Peter 2:22

Jesus is the **only mediator** between God and mankind.
- John 14:6
- 1 Timothy 2:3–6a

Jesus **offers life** to those who believe.
- 1 John 5:11–12

Jesus gave us His Holy Spirit to **empower us** to live for the glory to God.

- John 16:12–15
- Romans 8:9–11

Jesus **commanded us** to witness to the world and be salt and light.
- Matthew 5:13–16
- Matthew 28:16–20

Jesus **announced and revealed** the kingdom of God, which is our first citizenship.
- Luke 11:20, 19:11
- 1 Peter 2:9–17

## SALT AND LIGHT TACTICS

In light of these biblical truths, what does it mean to be "salt and light" in the world as an individual? Here are some basics I have tried to articulate and model in my life:

- **Make your witness to family and friends fundamentally about Jesus.** He is the issue. Not you, not me, not church, not Christian history, not ethical or philosophical systems. Not anything else. Jesus is the one focal deciding point in all of human history. Christianity is the only world religion based on a person, not a set of beliefs or recommended actions. Christianity rises and falls based on the question of Jesus' identity. Jesus said, "when I am lifted up from the earth, I will draw all people to myself" (John 12:32). As someone has said, Christianity is not about "do," it is about "done." Who Jesus is and what He has done for us is the core of the Good News.

- **Let your light shine so that God gets the glory.** Your life-witness is the seedbed for effective testimony. You can know the root by examining the fruit. Live your life in such a way that people are drawn to God through you. Matthew

5:16, "let your light shine before men, that they may see your good deeds and glorify your Father in Heaven." Put your life in high-beams that point to God!

- **Be a grace-filled person.** Do not allow yourself to be baited into hostility and anger. For many years, I was so full of "truth" and anxious to "beat" people in arguments that few people ever came to Jesus through me. Since then, I have tried to live and work in such a way as to allow the witness of my life and the grace of my speech be attractive and winsome to my environment. "Be wise in the way you act toward outsiders; make the most of every opportunity. Let your conversation be always full of grace, seasoned with salt, so that you may know how to answer everyone" (Colossians 4:5–7). You can lead a horse to water, but you can't make him drink—however, you can give him salt to make him thirsty! Grace is the salt of a believer's witness.

- **Be bold and gentle.** This used to be a "disconnect" for me. But I eventually learned it is possible to be both bold and gentle. In my role, I have had occasions as a student, pastor, and university president to have conversations with people of either many different faiths, no faith at all, and those antagonistic to Christianity and Christians. My experience is that we always need to ask the Holy Spirit to help us find ways to witness that are gentle, yet bold. Ask God to guide and direct your words. Silent witness must not be your only witness. "But in your hearts revere Christ as Lord. Always be prepared to give an answer to everyone who asks you to give the reason for the hope you have. But do this with gentleness and respect" (1 Peter 3:15–16). In other words, be bold in love!

It is my hope that the above guidance has been helpful to you as an individual. But for the remainder of this chapter, I want to discuss what it might look like for *the church* to live as "salt and light" in our world. If our biblical mandate is to engage with the world and live redemptively, inviting people to be reconciled to God in Christ, what does that look like in the various spheres of society? Living redemptively means that we should be known more for compassion than judgment, caring than criticism, hope instead of despair, and engagement rather than isolation. Sadly, many in the media and culture have painted exactly the opposite view of Christ-followers. Scripture tells us repeatedly what the character of God is and how that must be lived out in our world. Here are some foundational biblical texts to inform our corporate witness in the world:

> Righteousness and justice are the foundation of your throne; love and faithfulness go before you. (Psalm 89:14)

> Teacher, which is the greatest commandment in the Law? Jesus replied: "Love the Lord your God with all your heart and with all your soul and with all your mind." This is the first and greatest commandment. And the second is like it: "Love your neighbor as yourself." All the Law and the Prophets hang on these two commandments. (Matthew 22:36–40)

> Though I am free and belong to no one, I have made myself a slave to everyone, to win as many as possible. To the Jews I became like a Jew, to win the Jews. To those under the law I became like one under the law (though I myself am not under the

law), so as to win those under the law. To those not
having the law I became like one not having the
law (though I am not free from God's law but am
under Christ's law), so as to win those under the
law. To the weak I became weak, to win the weak.
I have become all things to all people so that by all
possible means I might save some. I do this for the
sake of the gospel, that I may share in its blessings.
(1 Corinthians 9:19–23)

The compelling witness of the people of God here on planet
earth must be to draw people to relationship with Jesus and live in
a redemptive fashion so that people can see, hear, and experience
the kingdom of God in the world around us. As we have repeatedly
said, Jesus' prayer that we would see the will of God take place "on
earth as it is in heaven" is a grant of ambassadorship to followers of
Jesus. How then should we live as the people of God in this season
and with an eye towards being "salt and light"?

As stated above, I have found that for me the clarity of witness
must be rooted in the primacy of Jesus Christ and His lordship.
Then, the overflow of that truth witness should be experienced in
every sphere of society. Os Guinness was again helpful to frame up
some of the issues in his book, *Renaissance*:

Put differently, the defining affirmation of faith for
the Christian as a follower of Jesus is that "Jesus is
Lord." The evangelical imperative is therefore that
every article of faith, every assumption of thought,
every Christian practice, and every Christian habit
and tradition pass muster under the searching
scrutiny of what Jesus announced and initiated in
the coming of his kingdom.

American Evangelicals, for example, basked briefly in the cultural sun after the collapse of Protestant liberalism in the 1960s, flexing their newfound political muscles and enjoying a surge of cultural attention when around a third of America claimed to be "born again"—only to squander the moment with what was commonly their truth-deficient "feel good" theology, sub-Christian politics, mindless evangelism, and a host of trendy chases after relevance that proved transient, worldly and unimpressive. Tellingly, the era of Evangelical prominence coincided with an era of moral degeneration in the nation, which it did nothing to halt. The movement has ended not surprisingly in, first, a suicidal dilution of the Christian faith, and, then, in a significant defection from the faith by those who were repulsed by such shallowness and folly.

In recent times American Evangelicals, in their foolish failure to learn from the mistakes of Protestant liberalism and their passionate desire to escape any taint from their recent fundamentalist past and to be "relevant" and "seeker sensitive," have largely forgotten the required doubleness or the deliberate ambivalence of this stance. Evangelicals little realize how much they have become the spiritual smiley button of suburban America.

Carl F. H. Henry, the great Evangelical theologian and leader, used to say of his fellow believers in the United States, "Earlier, it was next to impos-

sible to get Evangelicals out into the culture. Now
it is equally impossible to get the culture out of
Evangelicals." In its shallow and noisy worldliness,
much Evangelicalism has become little more than
the culture-religion of the declining Christian consensus that once dominated America.[1]

When we talk about the witness of the body of Christ in society,
we must not be incarnating a shallow and limited version of faith
witness. The body of Christ, gathered in community and scattered
as empowered ambassadors, must witness to the lordship of Jesus in
every dimension of society and culture.

Many years ago, the Lord began to challenge and chastise me
as a pastor that every believer had a kingdom assignment. Much
of my early experience in church life was a poor reflection of the
Reformation notion of the "priesthood of all believers." Function-
ally speaking, I had bought the lie that "really committed" Christians were pastors and missionaries, and everyone else was at a much
lower level. While I never would have expressed those words out
loud, the reality of how I often led in church might have caused
people to come to that conclusion. Thankfully, I was rescued from
that deception and increasingly have been advocating for almost
three decades for the Second Reformation that I referenced earlier.
I want to see an explosion of "grace distributed" in every sphere of
society. I'm dreaming of the church being a discipling and equipping
center as it incarnates what Ephesians 4 describes as the "equipping
of the saints for the work of ministry." I believe for, see, and want to
multiply Christ-followers in business, education, government, arts
and media, family, and church all testifying to a transformational
relationship and experience with Jesus Christ.

When followers of Jesus learn to bring heaven to earth, we
will see kingdom harvests of epic proportions! Oswald Chambers

said, "It is not a question of being saved from hell, but in being saved in order to manifest the Son of God in our mortal flesh."[2] Martin Luther said, "A gospel that does not deal with the issues of the day is not a gospel at all."[3] I believe that there are indicators across our culture that churches are beginning to engage with the various cultural spheres and utilizing a strategic orientation to do so. Os Hillman has provided a helpful framework in his book, *Change Agent*, about what will typify a Christ-follower going after a strategic kingdom assignment in their sphere of society:

1. **Excellence.** If we fail to do our work with excellence, we fail to earn the right to be a leader that others will look up to.

2. **Ethics and integrity.** Psalm 51 says God desires truth in the inward parts. Are you the same person in private as in public?

3. **Extravagant love and service.** Jesus said we must be servants just as He was. Serving others tangibly models the humility of Jesus.

4. **Signs and wonders.** Experiencing God's presence and power is what distinguishes you as a follower of Jesus. Are you manifesting His life in the area of your calling?[4]

I am praying and believing for a generation of discipled and Spirit-empowered followers of Jesus to invade every sphere of society, with the blessing and commissioning of their church leadership and community for the redemption of culture. I can see a day where American culture has a witness for Jesus in every domain, and the culture itself (including the media) is unable to see or shape a narrative other than followers of Jesus are the single greatest force for good and lovers of humanity on the planet. Our world is desperately in need of the light and life of the gospel. We have the opportunity to demonstrate that light and life by the way we love and live engaged in culture, not isolated from it.

Henry Blackaby wrote *Experiencing God* in 1990, and it has become a touchstone resource for millions as they journey forward in their faith experience. In an interview, he provided some amazing guidance for pastors, church leaders, and Christ-followers serving in various marketplaces of life. Though somewhat lengthy, it is worthy of our consideration as we ponder how pastors and leaders can disciple, equip, and release ambassadors into the world:

> "If someone were to ask me right now where do
> I sense the greatest potential for revival," he said,
> "I'd say in corporate America." Blackaby relates
> to about 170 CEOs of Fortune 100 and Fortune
> 500 companies, most of whom have read his
> book *Experiencing God*. After reading the book,
> all of them have requested a conference call with
> Blackaby to discuss their responses to the book.
> He has scheduled about ten different conference
> calls, with eight to ten of them on each call at one
> time. What is the major concern of these CEOs?
> Blackaby says, "They are asking me, 'How do we
> experience God in corporate America?'" He finds
> it much, much easier to guide corporate America
> than to guide the church community into fresh,
> new experiences with God.[5]

> I asked Dr. Blackaby why the local church has been
> so ineffective at equipping men and women in the
> workplace. "We need spiritual leaders to guide
> them. I find very few spiritual leaders understand

the role of the marketplace in the mind of God. I hear leaders speak, and they never address that issue. It is as if they are totally oblivious to the need to equip these leaders. When I preach on this and why they need to equip leaders in the marketplace, I get a tremendous response. If the churches ever taught the ways of God toward the marketplace, everything would be different. Right now, they are telling marketplace people to come and help them build their church. They have it backward. They are supposed to be equipping them for their role in the marketplace. When I tell them that, the lights come on. Many pastors repent when they realize they have it backwards. Churches totally turn around when they change their focus."[6]

"...having been built on the foundation of the apostles and prophets, Jesus Christ Himself being the chief cornerstone, in whom the whole building, being joined together, grows into a holy temple in the Lord in whom you also are being built together for a dwelling place of God in the Spirit." (Ephesians 2:20–22)

The local church is designed to be a Holy Spirit-training outpost for equipping God's people to be kingdom warriors of love and servanthood on earth and to destroy the works of darkness. Paul said the church would be established on the apostles and prophets with Jesus as the cornerstone. The natures of these two offices are worth noting. The office of prophet sees the reality of situations; prophets see what is coming and how to discern the times we live in. They discern the deceptive ways of the world system and speak absolute truth at the risk of persecution for the sake of upholding truth. The office of the apostle is defined as one who is "sent out" to establish foundations and build upon it. Apostles are to lay spiritual foundations so that the other three offices of pastor, evangelist, and teacher fill in the missing bricks to the foundation.[7]

I am believing for a complete return of the fivefold ministry of the church so that apostles, prophets, pastors, teachers, and evangelists will unleash a Spirit-empowered generation of Christ-followers to live redemptively as salt and light in their streams of ambassadorship and vocation. As we do, I am convinced that the church will also have to address specific cultural giants that have arisen and are residing in the land. Many of these giants are so entrenched in our culture that it will be miraculous to see or believe for any change at all. This is exactly why the church must engage and face these giants (for the glory of God!). Which giants to face and how to address them is the subject of our next chapter.

*four*

---

# THE FIVE GIANTS OF CULTURE TODAY

Remember, our goal is to believe and live for a prevailing church. The prevailing church will be engaged in society for cultural transformation so the heart and redemptive love of Christ will be manifested in the various spheres of society for the glory of God. While I have no expectation of the body of Christ becoming any form of political action group, I do believe in Christian political engagement and a strategic need for us to identify key issues about what we can engage to help define the moral center of our nation. Thankfully, there are several organizations already engaged in this type of work. (I've provided a list of them at the end of the chapter.) Christians can and must engage in the public square and do so with a winsome, redemptive, loving, and compassionate presence.

The history of the United States is rich with a Judeo-Christian foundation that provided the biblical and spiritual foundations for our laws and governing documents. (See the Afterword with some reference materials for further study in this area.) Areas of sin and national failure, like our toleration of slavery and injustice, are stains upon our heritage, but they are a failure to live up to our ideals not a repudiation of them. Our ideals proceed from the strong and secure base of the foundational documents of our nation, all of which are derived in substantive part from the Bible and the spiritual lives of our founders. The stewardship of our covenant heritage as the people of God is part of the awe-inspiring trust that we have received from those who have gone before us. In fact, one of my foundational commitments to the authority of Scripture and the heritage of our nation is a continued blessing of the nation of Israel. God's chosen people, Israel, continue to be part of His agenda for our world, and our prayers and support of our Jewish brothers and sisters help reiterate the value we place on the Jewish heritage we all have as followers of Jesus, the Jewish carpenter. (See israeladvocates.org, icfj.org, and cufi.org for additional resources to help with your study.)

Clarity about our foundations allows us to understand how God has been active in history and with society since the first pages of Scriptures. Here are a number of specific verses that help us frame up what our biblical hopes are for engaging with the society into which God has placed us:

> Those who forsake instruction praise the wicked, but those who heed it resist them. Evildoers do not understand what is right, but those who seek the LORD understand it fully. (Proverbs 28:4–5)

> When the righteous thrive, the people rejoice; when the wicked rule, the people groan. (Proverbs 29:2)

> He has shown you, O mortal, what is good. And

> what does the LORD require of you? To act justly
> and to love mercy and to walk humbly with your
> God. (Micah 6:8)

> I urge, then, first of all, that petitions, prayers,
> intercession and thanksgiving be made for all
> people—for kings and all those in authority, that
> we may live peaceful and quiet lives in all godli-
> ness and holiness. This is good, and pleases God
> our Savior, who wants all people to be saved and
> to come to a knowledge of the truth. (1 Timothy
> 2:1–4)

Following after the God of Scripture means that we live in such
a way for the righteous to thrive and we act with justice and mercy.
But today, there are many giants in the land opposing people of
faith. For our present age, I have selected five cultural giants that
I believe deserve "five smooth stones" of a prevailing church to
ensure our nation is protected and a greenhouse of kingdom health
can arise for generations to come. I recognize that these five giants
are not the only challenges in our society, but it is my hope that
they represent the five most critical so we can unify our resources to
ensure their defeat.

## The Five Cultural Giants of Our Time

1. **The giant of historical revisionism.** This giant often takes
   the guise of "history," as repeated projects attempt to undercut
   the spiritual and religious foundations of our nation. While we
   do not worship the Constitution, the Founders, or the Bible,
   we recognize that each of them is a gift from God. Without
   the Founders (and their predecessors, the Pilgrims and the

Puritans), the Constitution, and the Scriptures, the American experiment would never have happened. By virtually all accounts, the United States has been the most successful experiment in a republican form of government in human history with the greatest effects for the Great Commission that has ever existed. We are committed to biblical authority in life, and view our constitution as a stewardship trust so that we can see our nation bring glory to God through our national character.

My friend Len Munsil leads Arizona Christian University (arizonachristian.edu) and has written the book *Transforming Culture with Truth*. Munsil takes aim at the historical ignorance and apathy of most modern institutions when he quotes from Herb London, writing as follows:

> It is astonishing that those in the West are living through the near extinction of their civilization. For students in the academy today, the Western civilization history course, virtually a standard curriculum offering 30 years ago, has disappeared. This survey course covering classical antiquity to the present was the glue, the all-embracing narrative, that gave coherence to everything else the university taught. At the very least, students came away from this course with a partial recognition of their civilization and its monumental achievements.[1]

2. **The giant of abortion and euthanasia.** This giant regards human life as a commodity, expendable if social value or personal convenience is questioned or violated. It has ended the life of almost 60 million Americans since 1973 and repeatedly

cheapens the value of human life in the name of compassion or social utilitarianism. We are committed to treating all human life as precious and made in the image of God. We honor life in the womb and outside the womb until natural death.

It might seem that there is nothing more that could be written after almost fifty years of the battle here in the US, but actually more remains to be said. We have tolerated the murder of over sixty million babies since 1970. And while it might be possible to believe that this is a "cultural" problem and not a "church" problem, the data says otherwise. Instead of attempting to write a whole new section of information on this well-studied subject, I simply want to point you to a reference that will be helpful to you. My friend, Pastor Chip Ingram, provides an array of helpful abortion insights in his book *Culture Shock* that are worthy of review here:

> The fact is that 65 percent of all women who have abortions self-identify as Christians.[2]

> As I prepared this chapter, doing my best to look at this issue objectively, the statistic that most shocked me was learning that 65 percent of all women who have had abortions self-identify as Christians—35 percent Protestant, 28 percent Catholic. Tragically, 56 percent of all abortions are performed on women in their twenties and another 18 to 20 percent are performed on teenagers. So about 70 percent of all abortions are being performed on women age thirty and under.[3]

Planned Parenthood used to say that it was not a baby but a fetus, an unwanted pregnancy puts a woman at risk, and the woman is more important than the fetus. However, with the advent of advanced-image technology, it is almost impossible to deny that the child growing within is a human life. So, Planned Parenthood has more recently changed its messaging:

Today, when you read the extended literature from Planned Parenthood, they no longer use the term "fetus." They talk about a baby or a pre-born baby. The message is: "This is the new normal. It's unfortunate. We wish there weren't so many abortions, but for very specific reasons, we need to keep this a real option for women."[4]

An examination of early Church writings, especially the Didache, reveals passionate pleadings for the value of children and the value of life on the part of Christians. Because of the convictions of the early Church and the transformation of the culture, these practices were eliminated for the next fifteen hundred years.[5]

History can often turn our preconceptions upside down, and what occurred in the mid-to-late 1800s in the abortion debate is just such a story. The early 1800s found abortion illegal after 'quickening,' the time when a mother could feel the movement of her unborn child in the womb. But after 1840, as abortion became more acceptable for women and more lucrative for doctors, things began to change. The birthrate in the United States dropped from 7 to 3.5 children per family by the late 1800s, with abortion terminating one-fifth to one-third of all pregnancies. Abortion ads were numerous in both big and small newspapers.[6]

The early feminists decreed abortion as a violation of women's rights. The AMA and the women at the forefront of the feminist movement teamed up to enact laws that outlawed abortion in America.[7]

Take, for example, Elizabeth Cornwell, who is the executive director of the Richard Dawkins Foundation: "There's a war on the womb. As a secular pro-lifer, I believe my case is scientifically and philosophically sound. Science concedes that human life begins at fertilization, and it follows that abortion is ageism and discrimination against a member of our own species."[8]

3. **The giant of religious repression.** Unleashed across the country that was founded to secure religious freedom for its founders, the United States now plays host to a religious animus that is particularly pointed at Christianity. Further visibility of this giant has come through the increasing adoption and idealization of a socialist worldview that is the historic root of the slaughter of millions of people in the name of social progress. We are committed to religious liberty and believe that a socialist economic and political system is the greatest natural threat to religious liberty around the world.

As a university president, it gives me particular pain to know that college classrooms across the country are often the source for the socialism infection. College students today often become the teachers, and community and business leaders of tomorrow. Abraham Lincoln recognized the inherent challenge of this phenomenon when he stated, "The philosophy of the school room in one generation will be the philosophy of the government in the next."[9]

The anti-Christian bias of mainstream media, social media platform companies, and much of the cultural "intelligentsia" of our day, including film makers and artists, is well known and documented. However, rather than railing against those entities, I believe the greatest opportunity here exists for Christian creatives to engage with culture in an educated and well-grounded biblical worldview with an eye to redeem.

4.  **The giant of racism and injustice.** All humanity is created in the image of God, and we also are stained by the presence of sin. The giant of racism and injustice has often been experienced in our world and grows in strength when the people of God are silent or withdrawn from society and its problems. Scripture provides us in Ephesians 2, written to people with enmity and strife between them, with the most glorious view of racial and ethnic reconciliation and the prevailing church lives in light of our calling, not our circumstances. We are committed to living out the calling the Master has for the one human race and we live this as redeemed sons and daughters of His. Read these words and hear the call of the Savior:

> For he himself is our peace, who has made the
> two groups one and has destroyed the barrier,

the dividing wall of hostility, by setting aside in his flesh the law with its commands and regulations. His purpose was to create in himself one new humanity out of the two, thus making peace, and in one body to reconcile both of them to God through the cross, by which he put to death their hostility. He came and preached peace to you who were far away and peace to those who were near. For through him we both have access to the Father by one Spirit. Consequently, you are no longer foreigners and strangers, but fellow citizens with God's people and also members of his household, built on the foundation of the apostles and prophets, with Christ Jesus himself as the chief cornerstone. In him the whole building is joined together and rises to become a holy temple in the Lord. And in him you too are being built together to become a dwelling in which God lives by his Spirit. (Ephesians 2:14–22)

We are committed to a biblical experience of racial unity, justice, and the application of a biblical experience full of grace and truth to reform our healthcare, immigration, and criminal justice systems. We believe the silence and inactivity of the church to address the most pressing social problems of our day to be one of the primary reasons that cultural elites find it increasingly easy to dismiss people of faith. We are convinced that followers of Jesus, engaged in the primary issues of our day and against racism and injustice, will be able to model heaven and help shape solutions full of racial unity and justice. We long for Christ-followers to present biblically grounded, Spirit-empowered, and constitutionally-sensitive solutions to healthcare, immigration, criminal justice, and other seemingly intractable problems of our day. The cure for cancer, the keys to criminal justice reform, and the welcoming and legal solution for immigration should all come from the people of God as gifts to our society. We believe that the pages of Scripture cry out for the redeemed of the Lord to present a picture of redeemed humanity to the world around us that is consistent and compelling and stands in stark contrast to the divisive identity politics of our day.

5. **The giant of identity and family.** We believe that the attacks on marriage, family, sexuality, and gender identity are a highly weaponized tool of the enemy of our soul. Pain and sorrow have been the inheritance of a society that walks away from the building blocks of any successful civilization. We are committed to biblical views of gender, sexuality, marriage, and family where parents have the right and responsibility to protect children from harmful decisions and inputs. Often when Christians advocate for these positions, they are seen as longing for a return to a hazy version of the 1950s. That is unequivocally not true. Christians are advocating for what God has designed as best for humankind.

While we recognize that divorce occurs (in the church and in general society), we also know it is not God's best. All the data tells us that "Children raised by their married moms and dads commit less crime, have less premarital sex, and have fewer children out of wedlock than children of divorce."[10] Our culture stands at the edge of a precipice; so many fewer people are getting married (they are living together without marriage or staying single), and so many fewer are having children. We are risking our future social freedoms:

Childbirth is the ultimate act of hope in the future. If you're married, have faith and hope, and think of children as a duty and a blessing, then you'll probably have kids. If you're pessimistic and view human beings as parasites on the planet, wasteful carbon footprints, or a drag on your hip lifestyle, you might even think it's your duty not to have children, to abort the ones you would otherwise have, or at the least to have no more than one. Take a walk through some secular urban areas of Manhattan, San Francisco, and Seattle. You'll notice lots of dogs on leashes but not many babies in strollers. Some 41 percent of babies are aborted in New York City.[11]

I also recognize that homosexuality, bisexuality, and trans-sexualism are topics of intense debate and a massive part of "cancel culture" in our society. My views are not likely to be winsome to some of my friends in the public square. It has been my great joy to be in relationship with many people with whom I have substantial disagreement on these issues. Each and every time, I have sought to love and honor all persons as made in the image of God and have affirmed the redemptive and loving care of Jesus and His people for those with whom we disagree on these matters. Because of my commitment to Jesus and the authority of Scripture, I land squarely on what the clear teachings of Jesus, the Scriptures, and the church regarding sexual relationship as being designed for one man and one woman in a covenantal marriage relationship. There are many aspects of sexual orientation and gender identity subjects worthy of our comment, but for the sake of brevity, I will again refer you to Chip Ingram's excellent book,

*Culture Shock.* Here are a few quotes from that book that will serve you well:

> The only experience of Christianity many in the homosexual community have had is with angry, bigoted people, some who have even been violent in their rejection. The absolute love of God has been completely missing from too many encounters.[12]

> Within self-defined Christian circles, we have one group that champions the truth without love and another group that champions love without truth.[13]

> Studies by Johns Hopkins University, Albert Einstein College of Medicine, Evelyn Hooker, a pro-homosexual scientist, and Masters and Johnson all deny there's any genetic link. They agree that the connection between genetics and homosexuality is a wishful myth.[14]

> How do I say to someone I really care about, "Whatever you want to do is okay. It's fine that you may live only half as long as expected life spans. And I don't mind that, like a domino, what happens to you will affect other people." By the gay community's own reports, 24 percent of homosexual males reported having up to 100 partners in their lifetime. The Journal of Sex Research studied the profiles of 2,583 older homosexuals and reported an even greater number of partners."[15]

> Ultimately, it's not a lifestyle; it's a death-style. But this harsh and unpopular truth needs to be com-

municated in the same way and with the same kind of compassion we would use with someone who was dying.[16]

The Masters and Johnson study talks about a remarkable success rate among homosexuals leaving the lifestyle when they get helpful support: 79.1 percent have immediate success; 71 percent remain celibate from their homosexual lifestyle. The research and the Bible both say, "This is not a life sentence that cannot change."[17]

So what can we do? I believe that the call of our day is to be like David and take "five smooth stones" that the Lord provides and go after each one of these giants of culture. I can imagine churches across the country, and in every county, going after these giants one at a time and all at once. A church engaged in such a way, empowered by the Holy Spirit and confronting these evils of our present hour, will be a prevailing church.

I have long admired the pastoral work and writing of Dr. Jack Hayford, Pastor Emeritus of Church on the Way in Van Nuys, California. About twenty years ago, I asked for and received permission to modify Pastor Hayford's writing, but I provide this with tribute to him as the originator of the foundational thoughts that were part of this brief encouragement below. He has long been a father figure in the faith to me, both from a distance and in several personal experiences with him. I wrote this near the year 2000 and believe it still resonates today as the body of Christ lives out being salt and light in our world. As we go after the giants articulated above, I believe the church will call forth believers to be activated in society to slay these giants for the glory of God.

## EIGHT THINGS CHRISTIANS CAN DO FOR AMERICA

by Dr. John Jackson (c. 2000)
with thanks to Dr. Jack Hayford of Church on the Way,
Van Nuys, California

1.  **Believe the Promise.** "If my people, who are called by
    my name, will humble themselves and pray and seek my
    face and turn from their wicked ways, then will I hear from
    heaven, and I will forgive their sin and will heal their land."
    (2 Chronicles 7:14)

2.  **Bless Your Enemies.** "You have heard that it was said,
    'Love your neighbor and hate your enemy.' But I tell you,
    love your enemies and pray for those who persecute you."
    (Matthew 5:43–44)

3.  **Value Life.** "Speak up for those who cannot speak for
    themselves, for the rights of all who are destitute."
    (Proverbs 31:8)

4.  **Pursue Unity.** "My prayer is not for them alone. I pray also
    for those who will believe in me through their message,
    that all of them may be one, Father, just as you are in me
    and I am in you. May they also be in us so that the world
    may believe that you have sent me." (John 17:20–21)

5.  **Live in Purity.** "Do everything without grumbling or
    arguing, so that you may become blameless and pure,
    'children of God without fault in a warped and crooked
    generation.' Then you will shine among them like stars in
    the sky as you hold firmly to the word of life." (Philippians
    2:14–16a)

6. **Serve the Needy.** "In the same way, let your light shine before others, that they may see your good deeds and glorify your Father in heaven." (Matthew 5:16)

7. **Preserve Liberty.** "Now the Lord is the Spirit, and where the Spirit of the Lord is, there is freedom." (2 Corinthians 3:17)

8. **Share Christ with Passion.** "Therefore go and make disciples of all nations, baptizing them in the name of the Father and of the Son and of the Holy Spirit, and teaching them to obey everything I have commanded you. And surely I am with you always, to the very end of the age." (Matthew 28:19–20)

## ORGANIZATIONS FOR EDUCATION AND ENGAGEMENT:

Alliance Defending Freedom: www.adflegal.org
American Council for Evangelicals: www.theamericancouncil.org
California Family Council: www.californiafamily.org
Family Council: www.familycouncil.org
First Liberty: www.firstlibertylive.com
Focus on the Family: www.focusonthefamily.com
Foundations of Freedom: www.foundationsoffreedom.com
Pacific Justice Institute: www.pacificjustice.org

# five

# THE CHURCH I SEE

*"What does it feel like when people you wouldn't want as next door neighbors are now worshipping and praying with you?"* (Pastor's wife, personal conversation)

*"Pastor, I'm coming to your church. Cause if those people over there (points to folks in the lobby) can come here and find God, then there's something going on here that is life-changing."* (LifePoint Church in NV, personal conversation, circa 1999)

*"The greatest question of our time is not communism versus individualism, not Europe versus America, not even the East versus the West; it is whether men can live without God."* (Will Durant, noted historian)

The people of God have a master. The people of God have a calling. The people of God have heavenly ambassadorships that will lead them to manifest the presence and power of Christ by living in Spirit-empowered fashion in the respective domains within society. Men and women will be reached for Christ, become disciple-making disciples of Jesus, and will see the transformation of culture for the glory of God as they love, live, work, and vote in alignment with biblical values. It is the heart of God to see His people living on planet earth as heavenly ambassadors who have been equipped by apostles, prophets, evangelists, pastors, and teachers to serve Christ in their spheres.

I have had the honor of working with researcher and writer Ed Stetzer at various events. Ed, who is now at a sister institution, Wheaton College, provides great clarity about what this kingdom life is all about in his powerful book, *Subversive Kingdom*. He writes:

> The kingdom of God is a radical rejection of every value or point of view that keeps people in bondage to untruth, blinded to Christ's mercy.[1]

> This is not open warfare. Jesus did not march on Rome. He never called together a zealot army. He never wrote a political manifesto. He simply announced that because he had come, the kingdom had come—and it would move out from Jerusalem in surprising ways. Not by might but by the subterfuge of lives lived for King Jesus.[2]

> Because that's just how the kingdom works. Pushing back the darkness and shining the light of God's love into unexpected places is kingdom activity. Drawing people toward the redeeming grace of Jesus Christ and into genuine, saving relationship with him is the kingdom result.[3]

> Through Jesus' teaching and preaching, he was proclaiming to everyone that they could be

part of God's agenda on earth by repenting and believing, that this "kingdom of heaven" was primarily spiritual in nature. And through his miracles of healing, he was making visibly evident his authoritative power over the curse of our fallen, helpless condition. After all, "Which is easier: to say to the paralytic, 'Your sins are forgiven,' or to say, 'Get up, pick up you mat and walk'?" (Mark 2:9). They're both easy when your power as King is supreme over every part of the rebellious world, both physical and spiritual.[4]

To be in the kingdom is amazing. To live for the kingdom is indescribably joy. A joy you can't get enough of.[5]

C.S. Lewis in *The Weight of Glory*: We are half-hearted creatures, fooling around with drink and sex and ambition when infinite joy is offered us, like an ignorant child who wants to go on making mud pies in a slum because he cannot imagine what is meant by the offer of a holiday at the sea. We are far too easily pleased.[6]

What Ed helps us to capture is how absolutely necessary and essential it is to understand "kingdom" in contrast with the world we inhabit "normally." The normal US experience of flowing with the cultural stream will not result in a kingdom-of-God life. Matthew 7 tells us that the "kingdom way" is a narrow way and we must walk that road carefully following the Master.

So, we end this book with how we began… "how should we then live"? As believers organized in churches/ekklesias, how can we live out the call of God upon our lives? Or put another way, as

Samuel Shoemaker asked in the middle of the twentieth century, "Can your kind of church change this kind of world?"[7]

I believe, and am staking the rest of my life on this planet, that Jesus' people can be discipled and equipped by the fivefold ministry, becoming authentic Jesus-following and reproducing disciple-makers who live in society for the glory of God.

I see a church with groups of believers who are launched, like aircraft from a strategic vessel, targeted to their specific assignments in culture and community. (See Stephen Johnson's description of this model at www.thefreedomoutpost.net.)

I see a church engaged in society, with redemptive love, full of grace and truth, contending for what heaven on earth looks like in the critical issues of our day.

I see assemblies of believers in all three thousand counties of the United States living for the glory of God and following Jesus with radical love, radical truth, and radical grace.

I see the church prevailing against the darkness of our day. I see the church defeating the enemy of our souls and recognizing him as the thief, liar, and murderer that he is (John 10:10).

I see the church living fully armored up, recognizing that we are not in a country club; we are not called to survive the prison camp until we get rescued—we are called to defeat the enemy in a very real war (Ephesians 6).

I see the church taking up its birthright, responding to its Master and calling, and living in a prevailing fashion.

I see the church that Jesus loves, loving the world He died for, and living for the kingdom He ushered onto our planet.

I see the Savior, His bride, His kingdom, and His will being done "on earth, as it is in heaven."

*Even so, Maranatha (come quickly, Lord)!*

# RELIGIOUS FOUNDATIONS
# OF OUR NATION

For many people in our nation, the idea that America was founded as a "Christian nation" or even that it was founded with "Judeo-Christian" values is a controversial notion. Historical events and their retelling in our modern era have caused many to wonder if there is anything about our nation to be celebrated. As I write in 2020, statues of historical figures have been destroyed across the country, Project 1619 has recast the entire American experience as birthed and lived through slavery, and a host of academic institutions and cultural settings have all but decreed that America is evil and must be replaced, likely with a socialist and secular state.

I say *no* to that. And, I believe that Scripture and American history say *no* to that as well.

Many long books have been written chronicling the subject of America's religious heritage. And while I have written and communicated previously in this book that I believe our national history (and present!) is full of terrible sins and shortcomings, I reject any notion that America is anything other than a tremendous reservoir of blessing with a sacred trust of stewardship to guard and enlarge the freedoms we have been given.

For the sake of the reader who may desire, I have provided a number of quotes and reference materials here that can help in your study of our heritage. My hope and prayer is that they encourage your heart, strengthen your mind, and steady your spirit as you participate in creating an even more blessed future for our nation, children, and grandchildren.

# QUOTES AND RESOURCES

George Washington, first president of United States, said these words:

> Let my heart, gracious God, be so affected with Your glory and majesty that I may discharge those weighty duties which thou requires of me again. I have called on thee for pardon and forgiveness of sins for the sacrifice of Jesus Christ, offered on the cross for me, now gave us his son to die for me and has given me assurance of my salvation.

Some researchers at the University of Houston collected and reviewed over 15,000 documents from the early founders of our nation, the Founding Fathers, and they looked through their correspondence. They were trying to say, who were our early founding fathers most influenced by? Who did they quote? What were the sources? This is what they found. In the correspondence of the Founding Fathers, as they were writing back to each other, getting ready to write the Declaration of Independence, the Federalist Papers, and the Constitution of United States, 94 percent of their quotes came from the Bible.

## FROM *THE NAKED PUBLIC SQUARE* BY RICHARD NEUHAUS:

What is relatively new is the naked public square. The naked public square is the result of political doctrine and practice that would exclude religion and religiously grounded values from the conduct of public business. The doctrine is that America is a secular society. It finds dogmatic expression in the ideology of secularism. I will argue that the doctrine is demonstrably false and the dogma exceedingly dangerous.[1]

The case can be made that the great social and political devastations of our century have been perpetrated by regimes of militant secularism, notably those of Hitler, Stalin, and Mao. That is true, and it suggests that the naked public square is a dangerous place. When religious transcendence is excluded, when the public square has been swept clean of divisive sectarianisms, the space is opened to seven demons aspiring to transcendent authority.[2]

Thus the courts venture where politicians fear to tread. An outstanding instance of this was the Dred Scott decision of 1857, excluding slaves from the protection of the Constitution. That decision did not "take" democratically; it did not resolve but only exacerbated the issue it intended to settle. In that case, the issue was only resolved by civil war carried on by means of civil war.[3]

Yet more recently, the court rushed in where politicians had been tromping all over the issue. In Roe v. Wade (1973) the court "settled" the debate over abortion law by the apparently simple expedient of suspending all relative to the protection of the unborn. As John Noonan, professor of jurisprudence at the University of California, has noted, this is an audacious experiment without precedent in the law of any Western nation. As many others have noted, the failure of Roe v. Wade to be ratified by public consensus invokes the memory of the Dred Scott decision.[4]

Most people who have paid much attention to the phenomenon called democracy allow that its historical roots are somehow related to biblical religion. Most, but not all. Some textbook tellings of democracy's story attribute the whole idea to classical Greece. In this version, the influence of Christianity was entirely negative. Religion as the enemy of democratic freedom is epitomized, it is said, in the Inquisition. The classic period and our modern era of enlightenment are the opposite of everything represented by the Inquisition. Those who tell the story this way overlook the fact that in three hundred years the inquisition had fewer victims than were killed any given afternoon during the years of Stalin's purges and Hitler's concentration camps. Nonetheless, it is asserted that the modern era is uniquely friendly to democratic freedom. Christianity, it is said, was responsible for the unrelieved darkness of the Middle Ages. The darkness was only broken by the dawning of the Renaissance in the fourteenth and fifteenth centuries.[5]

He observes that many of the founding fathers believed in God and cited other instances in which the state continues to recognize religion. The conclusion: It can be truly said therefore, that today, as in the beginning, our national life reflects a religious people who, in the words of Madison, are "earnestly praying, as... in duty bound, that the Supreme Lawgiver of the Universe...guide them into every measure which may be worthy of his [blessing]."[6]

We earlier took note of statements of John Adams and others to the effect that a notion of limited government, such as ours, assumes that the business of values and culture is being taken care of "elsewhere." Throughout most of our history, the proposition that ours is a nation "under God."[7]

What is frequently meant by pluralism today is a legalized secular distortion of Judeo-Christian concern for the marginal.[8]

## From *Not a Day Care* by Everett Piper:

This is not a day care. This is a university.[9]

Today's law students are tomorrow's lawyers and judges—and if you wonder why so many judges legislate from the bench, take a look at what they teach in law school. Today's business students are tomorrow's business leaders—and if you wonder why so many corporations are so politically correct, take a look at what they teach at business school. The students who want to ban Plato, Aristotle, Voltaire, and Kant from college curricula will soon be sitting on school boards or serving in academia.

The students who believe in shutting down unpopular and often conservative points of view will soon be leading our state legislatures. What is taught in the classroom today will be practiced in the real world tomorrow.[10]

How did we get, after all, from the Greatest Generation—meeting the challenges of an economic depression, World War II, the Korean War, and the Cold War—to the Most Self-Absorbed Generation in need of safe spaces and trigger warnings? Much of the fault lies with education, and what happened to higher education in the 1960s. The student riots of that era led to three major, and harmful, developments: one, the purpose of college became less about learning and more about flattering the self-righteousness of students; two, the core curriculum of classics was gutted as the allegedly irrelevant or oppressive works of dead, white, males and were replaced by more "relevant" topics like women's studies and various ethnic studies, all informed by cultural Marxism; and three, many of the campus radicals of the 1960s became tenured professors and transformed their academic departments in their own image.[11]

Good education, a truly liberal education, one engaged in respectful debate and the search for truth, relies on the idea that there is a truth out there to be grasped, whether in a mathematical formula, a scientific discovery, a philosophical thesis, or a literary work that highlights a truth about the laws of nature or the nature of man.[12]

It is a common error of youth. "The arrogance of the young is a direct result of not having known enough consequences," said humorist Harry Golden. "The turkey that every day greedily approaches the farmer who tosses him grain is not wrong. It is just that no one ever told him about Thanksgiving." So it is with millennials who arrogantly presume they know all that is relevant about reality at such a young age.[13]

Yale was established by the Church. Led by the Reverend James Pierpont, it declared its purpose: "To plant and under ye Divine blessing to propagate in this Wilderness, the blessed Reformed, Protestant Religion, in ye purity of its Order and Worship." Its students were required to "live religious, godly and blameless lives according to the rules of God's Word, diligently reading the Holy Scriptures, the fountain of light and truth; and constantly attend upon the duties of religion, both in public and secret." Prayer was a requirement. Princeton's early presidents included some of America's foremost religious leaders, including revivalist preacher Jonathan Edwards and John Witherspoon, a signer of the Declaration of Independence. Its purpose could not have been clearer: "Cursed is all learning that is contrary to the cross of Christ." Seven of the eight Ivy League institutions were founded in like manner to train up future generations in a biblical ethic; to educate a moral citizenry, and, thus, lay the foundation for a free people and a free nation. Dartmouth was founded to 'Christianize' the native American tribes and its motto even to this day is Vox clamantis in deserto: "The voice of one crying in the wilderness." Evangelist George Whitfield originally conceived the University of Pennsylvania. Three-fourths of its original trustees were affiliated with the Church of England. Its motto is Leges Sine Moribus Vanae: "Laws without morals [are] useless"' Brown University was founded by Baptists with the motto, In Deo Speramus which means "In God We Hope." Columbia University was inspired by the dream of Colonel Lewis Morris, who wrote a letter to the Society for the Propagation of the Gospel in Foreign Parts, the missionary arm of the Church of England, arguing that new York City was an ideal community in which to establish a college for such purposes. The university's motto is taken directly from Psalm 36:9, In lumine Tuo videbimus lumen: "In Thy light we shall see light."[14]

Rev. George W. Rutler, pastor of St. Michael's Church in New York City, recognized the cultural impact of our pampering: The average age of a Continental soldier in the American Revolution was one year less than that of a college freshman today. Alexander Hamilton was a fighting lieutenant-colonel when 21, not to mention Joan of Arc who led an army into battle and saved France when she was about as old as an American college sophomore. In our Civil War, eight Union generals and seven Confederate generals were under the age of 25. The age of most U.S. and RAF fighter pilots in World War II was about that of those on college junior varsity teams. Catholics who hoped in this election for another Lepanto miracle will remember that back in 1571, Don Juan of Austria saved Western civilization as commanding admiral when he was 24. None of these figures, in the various struggles against the world and the flesh and devil, retreated to safe spaces weeping in the arms of grief therapists.[15]

"If fascism ever comes to America," Ronald Reagan told Mike Wallace in 1975, "it will come in the name of liberalism." Indeed, ideological fascism has come in place of academic freedom, waiving the banners of trigger warnings, microaggressions, and safe spaces on college campuses across the land. You must submit. You must agree. You must comply with the fasces—the acceptable bundle of ideas—or [sic] you will be silenced and expelled.[16]

# FROM *A FREE PEOPLES SUICIDE* BY OS GUINNESS:

Augustine of Hippo argued that the best way to define a people is by their "loved thing held in common," or what it is they love supremely.[17]

But unless sustained, freedom could also prove to be America's idol—something trusted ultimately that cannot bear ultimate weight.[18]

Unfettered freedom could prove to be the Achilles' heel of the modern world, dissipating into license, triviality, corruption and a grand undermining of all authority, but for the moment the world is still both thrilled and enthralled by the great Age of Freedom. It is the Western world's most stunning success, and the United States is its proudest exemplar."[19]

The problem is not wolves at the door but termites in the floor. Powerful free people die only by their own hand, and free people have no one to blame but themselves. What the world seems fascinated to watch but powerless to stop is the spectacle of a free people's suicide."[20]

In the term that Tocqueville made famous later, freedom for Captain Preston and countless more like him was a habit of the heart, and it was kept strong by symbols and icons such as the Liberty Tree, the Liberty Bell and later the Stars and Stripes and the Statue of Liberty, rather than simply by books and declarations. As freeborn Englishmen, the colonists saw freedom as their birthright and as natural as their mother's milk and the New England air they breathed-even if they had to contend for it against their mother country. When Tocqueville witnessed a Fourth of July celebration in Albany, New York, in 1831, he observed, "It seemed that an electric current made the hearts vibrate."[21]

There are three tasks in establishing a free society that hopes to remain free-winning freedom, ordering freedom and sustaining freedom-and each was a prominent consideration to the American founders.[22]

The Declaration of Independence is not only an American document. It follows on the Magna Carta and the Bill of Rights as the third great title-deed in which the liberties of the English-speaking people are founded.[23]

Freedom requires a framework of order, which means restraint, yet the only restraint proper to freedom is self-restraint, which freedom undermines.[24]

Jefferson, for example, for all his dislike of England, held that Francis Bacon, Isaac Newton and John Locke were "the three greatest men that have ever lived, without any exception," and he hung their portraits as his heroes in his study at Monticello. Equally, the works of Plato, Aristotle, Thucydides, Polybius, Cicero, Virgil, Horace and Seneca were as common in the speeches of the founding generation as they were in their libraries.[25]

A constitution rests on a foundation. Or more accurately, it rests on a bedding of customs, traditions and moral standards, from which it grows and by which it is sustained. So the character and health of these customs is crucial, for some customs are positive, healthy and therefore supportive of the constitution, and others are negative, degenerate and hostile. "Desirable" customs make the private lives of citizens virtuous and the public character of the state "civilized and just," whereas "objectionable" customs are damaging.[26]

George Washington truly was "the indispensable man" of the American Revolution, as historian James Flexner described him, and he was so by force of his character rather than his ideas or his eloquence. In this and other similar incidents, he was a one-man check and balance on the abuse of power, and decisively so well before the Constitution framed the principle in law.[27]

Two things have consistently surprised me in my years in the United States: that the sole American answer to how freedom can be sustained is the Constitution and its separation of powers and that the rest of the founders' solution is now almost completely ignored.[28]

Benjamin Franklin made a terse statement: "Only a virtuous people are capable of freedom." Or as he stated it negatively in his famous maxims: "No longer virtuous, no longer free; is a maxim as true with regard to a private person as a Commonwealth."[29]

Lincoln's noble words engraved on the wall of his memorial next to him as he sits on his consuls' chair. The torrents of blood "drawn with the sword" in the Civil War, he concluded gravely, were to balance the books on account of "every drop of blood drawn with the lash" of 250 years of slavery. The terrible carnage of the blues and the grays was the severe price paid for the denial of the Declaration of Independence's promise of liberty for all.[30]

## FROM *LIBERTY'S SECRETS* BY JOSHUA CHARLES:

There alone, in the totality, do we discover the truth observed by Alexis de Tocqueville, one of America's most ardent admirers (and stridently friendly critics), that "Revolution in the United States was the result of a mature and thoughtful taste for freedom, and not a vague and ill-defined feeling for independence. It was not based upon the passions of disorder, but on the contrary love of order and the law directed its course.[31]

Charles writes that in their own contemporary context, the Founding Fathers did not think to pursue this ideal now called the "American Dream." Rather, founders like George Washington aspired for something far more personal and intimate: to be "under [their] own vine and fig."[32]

This concept can be traced back to Micah 4:4, where the speaker was describing a time where every man could find contentment on his land and freedom individually, without interference from others. The Founding Fathers wished for a time where a man could "exercise his liberty...in a morally responsible way so as to reap the fruits of his own labor and talents," something that would come once a person had found his purpose and began to enjoy life, liberty, and the pursuit of happiness. In other words, the "American dream" of the

Founders was intended *to unleash the full power of human potential so as to enable human flourishing to the greatest possible extent.*[33]

Notice that Douglass explicitly praised the Founders, Washington in particular, but heaped curses on the generation that followed the Founders. He continued: "Standing with God and the crushed and bleeding slave on this occasion, I will, in the name of humanity which is outraged, in the name of liberty which is fettered, in the name of the Constitution and the Bible, which are disregarded and trampled upon, dare to call in question and to denounce, with all the emphasis I can command, everything that serves to perpetuate slavery—the great sin and shame of America."[34]

[Frederick Douglass] concluded his thoughts on the Founders with an exhortation on the Constitution: But I differ from those who charge this baseness on the framers of the Constitution of the United States. It is a slander upon their memory, at least, so I believe... interpreted as it ought to be interpreted, the Constitution is a GLORIOUS LIBERTY DOCUMENT. Read its preamble, consider its purposes. Is slavery among them? It is at the gateway? Or is it in the temple? It is neither... [I]f it be not somewhat singular that, if the Constitution were intended to be, by its framers and adopters, a slave-holding instrument, why neither slavery, slaveholding, nor slave can anywhere be found in it... Now, take the Constitution according to its plain reading, and I defy the presentation of a single pro-slavery clause in it. On the other hand it will be found to contain principles and purposes entirely hostile to the existence of slavery.[35]

Tocqueville thus predicted, with stunning accuracy, many of the very same things our Founders predicted would happen in our society as we abandoned their founding principles:

1.  There would be a decline in education, knowledge, and the rise of a generally ignorant citizenry.

2.  There would be a loss of morality and a resulting rise in cultural narcissism.

3.  Society would develop an excessive love of material pleasures and prosperity, which both result from and further exacerbate the decline of morality.

4.  The Constitution would be intentionally misinterpreted so as to avoid the difficult process of amending it; thus, the limits it placed on the government would become essentially meaningless by the arbitrary redefinition of words.

5.  Once these false interpretations of the Constitution gained ground, the government would continue to grow faster and faster, as it would no longer be confined by its previous boundaries.

6.  Political parties would encourage and stoke the latent divisions in society to maintain and increase their power.

7.  With the expansion of the state beyond its constitutionally mandated boundaries, there would be rise in administrative tyranny. This occurs as government becomes more corporatized and amalgamated with

financial institutions, incentivizing the devaluation of our currency through fiat money printed by banks.

8. All of the previous points combine to create a monumental problem of debt as government expenses would rise in response to both the need to pay off its allies and sycophants, as well as the greater and greater demands on the public treasury by the citizenry itself.[36]

As alluded to in chapter 3, two of the greatest limitations placed on the power of the federal government were its enumerated powers and federalism.[37]

Jefferson wrote: I see, as you do, and with the deepest affliction, the rapid strides with which the federal branch of our government is advancing towards the usurpation of all the rights reserved to the States, and the consolidation in itself of all powers, foreign and domestic; and that, too, by constructions which, if legitimate, leave no limits to their power... Under the power to regulate commerce, they assume indefinitely that also over agriculture and manufactures, and call it regulation to take the earnings of one of these branches of industry, and that too the most depressed, and put them into the pockets of the other, the most flourishing of all... and aided by a little sophistry on the words "general welfare," a right to do, not only the acts to effect that, which are specifically enumerated and permitted, but whatsoever they shall think, or pretend will be for the general welfare. He concluded: Their younger recruits, who, having nothing in them of the feelings or principles of '76, now look to a single and splendid government of an aristocracy, founded on banking institutions, and moneyed incorporations under the guise and cloak of their favored branches of manufactures, commerce and navigation, riding and ruling over the plundered ploughman and beggared yeomanry. This will be to them a next best blessing to the monarchy of their first aim, and perhaps the surest stepping-stone to it.[38]

## FROM ERIC TEETSEL, PATHEOS.COM:

Religious freedom is the right to ask questions of ultimate significance and live in the light of the answers. It consists of an unconstrained mind and unconstrained body: the freedom of orthodoxy, belief consistent with doctrine, and of orthopraxy, behavior that conforms with one's beliefs. Conforming mind and body to one's most deeply held beliefs is a basic human right, worth of utmost protection. For this reason, religious freedom is America's "first freedom."[39]

# · NOTES ·

## INTRODUCTION

1   "prevailing," Dictionary.com, https://www.dictionary.com/browse/prevailing?s=t. Accessed 12/8/20.

## CHAPTER 1

1   Dave Kinnaman and Gabe Lyons, *unChristian: What a New Generation Really Thinks about Christianity...and Why It Matters* (Grand Rapids, MI: Baker Books, 2007), 42. Quoted in *The Outsider Interviews: A New Generation Speaks Out on Christianity* by Jim Henderson, Todd Hunter, and Craig Spinks (Grand Rapids, MI: Baker Books, 2012), 94.

2   Kinnaman and Lyons, *unChristian*, 47.

3   Kinnaman and Lyons, *unChristian*, 48.

4   Os Hillman, *Change Agent* (Lake Mary, Florida: Charisma House, 2011), 12.

5   Hillman, *Change Agent*, 14.

6   Kinnanman and Lyons, *unChristian*, 174.

7   Os Guinness, "Knowing Means Doing: A Challenge to Think Christianly," *Where Faith Meets Culture: A Radix Magazine Anthology*, vol. 20, No. 1 (Eugene, OR: Cascade Books, 2010), 40.

8   Terry Crist, *Learning the Language of Babylon: Changing the World by Engaging the Culture* (Chosen Books, 2001), 35.

9   Crist, *Learning the Language of Babylon*, 101.

10  Dave Hunt, "Christian Activism: Is It Biblical?" The Berean Call, November 1, 1989. https://www.thebereancall.org/content/christian-activism-it-biblical. Accessed December 11, 2020.

11  Hillman, *Change Agent*, xi.

12  Hillman, *Change Agent*, 8.

13  Hillman, *Change Agent*, 9.

14  Hillman, *Change Agent*, 10.

15  Ibid.

## CHAPTER 2

1   Colonel V. Donor, *The Samaritan Strategy: A New Agenda for Christian Activism* (Wolgemuth & Hyatt, 1998), 128.

2   Os Guinness, *Renaissance: The Power of the Gospel However Dark the Times* (Downers Grove, IL: InterVarsity Press, 2014), 62.

## CHAPTER 3

1   Os Guinness, *Renaissance*, 137.

2   Hillman, *Change Agent*, 25.

3   Hillman, *Change Agent*, 27.

4   Hillman, *Change Agent*, 168.

5   Hillman, *Change Agent*, 191.

6   Ibid.

7   Hillman, *Change Agent*, 191, 193.

## CHAPTER 4

1   Len Munsil, *Transforming Culture with Truth* (Arizona Christian University Press, 2015), 84.

2   Chip Ingram, *Culture Shock: A Biblical Response to Today's Most Divisive Issues* (Grand Rapids, MI: Baker Books, 2014), 134.

3  Ingram, *Culture Shock*, 150.

4  Ingram, *Culture Shock*, 139.

5  Ingram, *Culture Shock*, 143.

6  Ibid.

7  Ingram, *Culture Shock*, 144.

8  Ingram, *Culture Shock*, 148.

9  James Robison and Jay Richards, *Indivisible: Restoring Faith, Family, and Freedom Before It's Too Late* (New York City: Faith Words, 2012), 135.

10  Robison and Richards, *Indivisible*, 121.

11  Robison and Richards, *Indivisible*, 133.

12  Ingram, *Culture Shock*, 85.

13  Ingram, *Culture Shock*, 87.

14  Ingram, *Culture Shock*, 98.

15  Ingram, *Culture Shock*, 107.

16  Ingram, *Culture Shock*, 109.

17  Ingram, *Culture Shock*, 123.

## CHAPTER 5

1  Ed Stetzer, *Subversive Kingdom: Living as Agents of Gospel Transformation* (Nashville: B&H Publishing, 2012), 8.

2  Stetzer, *Subversive Kingdom*, 9.

3  Stetzer, *Subversive Kingdom*, 12.

4  Stetzer, *Subversive Kingdom*, 15.

5  Stetzer, *Subversive Kingdom*, 44.

6  Stetzer, *Subversive Kingdom*, 48.

7  George Hunter III, *Radical Outreach: Recovery of Apostolic Ministry and Evangelism* (Nashville: Abingdon Press, 2003), 74.

## AFTERWORD

1  Richard John Neuhaus, *The Naked Public Square: Religion and Democracy in America*, 2nd edition (Wm. B. Eerdmans Publishing Co.: 1988), ix.

2   Neuhaus, *Naked Public Square*, 8.

3   Neuhaus, *Naked Public Square*, 26.

4   Ibid.

5   Neuhaus, *Naked Public Square*, 94.

6   Neuhaus, *Naked Public Square*, 101.

7   Neuhaus, *Naked Public Square*, 138.

8   Neuhaus, *Naked Public Square*, 147.

9   Everett Piper, *Not a Daycare: The Devastating Consequences of Abandoning Truth* (Wash. D.C., Regnery Faith, 2017), 4, 5.

10  Piper, *Not a Daycare*, 9.

11  Piper, *Not a Daycare*, 32.

12  Piper, Not a Daycare, 34.

13  Piper, Not a Daycare, 35.

14  Piper, Not a Daycare, 71–72.

15  Piper, Not a Daycare, 106–7.

16  Piper, Not a Daycare, 191.

17  Os Guinness, *A Free Peoples Suicide: Sustainable Freedom and the American Future* (Downers Grove: InterVarsity Press, 2012), 16.

18  Guinness, *A Free Peoples Suicide*, 17.

19  Guinness, *A Free Peoples Suicide*, 18.

20  Guinness, *A Free Peoples Suicide*, 37.

21  Guinness, *A Free Peoples Suicide*, 43.

22  Ibid.

23  Guinness, *A Free Peoples Suicide*, 46.

24  Guinness, *A Free Peoples Suicide*, 61.

25  Guinness, *A Free Peoples Suicide*, 70.

26  Guinness, *A Free Peoples Suicide*, 79.

27  Guinness, *A Free Peoples Suicide*, 95.

28  Guinness, *A Free Peoples Suicide*, 96.

29  Guinness, *A Free Peoples Suicide*, 109.

30  Guinness, *A Free Peoples Suicide*, 200.

31  Joshua Charles, *Liberty's Secrets: The Lost Wisdom of America's Founders* (Wash. D.C., WND Books, 2015), xvi.

32  Charles, *Liberty's Secrets*, 185.

33  Charles, *Liberty's Secrets*, 186.

34  Charles, *Liberty's Secrets*, 224.

35  Charles, *Liberty's Secrets*, 225.

36  Charles, *Liberty's Secrets*, 232.

37  Charles, *Liberty's Secrets*, 247.

38  Charles, *Liberty's Secrets*, 259.

39  Eric Teetsel, "Religious Freedom in 10 Minutes," Patheos. com, September 27, 2013. https://www.patheos.com/ blogs/manhattanproject/2013/09/religious-freedom-in-10-minutes/. Accessed December 14, 2020.

# · BIBLIOGRAPHY ·

Barnett, Matthew. *The Church That Never Sleeps*. Nelson, 2000.

Bennett, William. *The De-Valuing of America*.
Harper Collins Christian, 1994.

Blackaby, Henry. *Experiencing God*. B & H Publishing Group, 1990.

Bloom, Allan. *The Closing of the American Mind*. Simon & Schuster, 1987.

Bork, Robert H. *Slouching Towards Gomorrah*. Harper Collins, 1996.

Carter, Stephen. *The Culture of Disbelief*. Basic Books, 1993.

Colson, Chuck. *How Now Shall We Live?* Tyndale House, 1999.

Colson, Chuck. *Kingdoms in Conflict*. Zondervan, 1987.

Charles, Joshua. *Liberty's Secrets*. WND Books, 2015.

Corvina, John and Anderson, Ryan T. and Girgis, Sherif. *Debating Religious Liberty and Discrimination*. Oxford University Press, 2017.

Crist, Terry. *Learning the Language of Babylon*. Chosen Books, 2001.

Dockery, David S. and Stonestreet, John. *Life, Marriage, and Religious Liberty*. Fidelis Books, 2019.

Donor, Colonel V. *The Samaritan Strategy*. Wolgemuth & Hyatt, 1988.

Dreher, Rod. *Live Not By Lies*. Sentinel, 2020.

Dreher, Rod. *The Benedict Option*. Sentinel, 2017.

George, Robert P. *Conscience and Its Enemies*. ISI Books, 2013.

Grudem, Wayne. *Politics According to The Bible*. Zondervan Academic, 2010

Greer, Peter and Horst, Chris. *Mission Drift*. Bethany House Publishers, 2014.

Guinness, Os. *A Free People's Suicide*. InterVarsity Press, 2012.

Guinness, Os. *Renaissance*. InterVarsity Press, 2014.

Henderson, Jim, Hunter, Todd, and Spinks, Craig. *The Outsider Interviews*. Baker Books, 2010.

Hewitt, Hugh. *Hugh Hewitt's Little Red Book*. Simon & Schuster, 2017.

Hillman, Os. *Change Agent*. Charisma House, 2011.

Holy Bible. *New International Version*. 1984.

Hunt, Dave. "Christian Activism: Is It Biblical?" The Berean Call, 1989.

Hunter, George G. *Radical Outreach*. Abingdon Press, 2003.

Ingram, Chip. *Culture Shock*. Baker Books, 2014.

Kinnaman, Dave and Gabe Lyons. *unChristian*. Baker Books, 2012.

Lewis, Robert. *The Church of Irresistible Influence*. Zondervan, 2001.

Lyons, Gabe. *The Next Christians*. Doubleday Religion, 2010.

Marsden, George M. *Fundamentalism and American Culture*. Oxford University Press, 1980.

Mohler, R. Albert. *The Gathering Storm*. Thomas Nelson, 2020.

Munsil, Len. *Transforming Culture with Truth*. Arizona Christian University Press, 2015.

Neuhaus, Richard John. *The Naked Public Square*. Eerdmans, 1988.

Niehbuhr, Rheinhold. *Christ and Culture*. Harper & Row, 1975.

Piper, Everett. *Not a Day Care*. Regnery Faith, 2017.

Reno, R.R. *Resurrecting the Idea of a Christian Society*. Regnery Faith, 2016.

Richards, Jay. *Money, Greed, and God*. Harper One, 2010.

Robison, James and Richards, Jay. *Indivisible*. Faith Words, 2012.

Rusaw, Rick and Swanson, Eric. *The Externally Focused Church*. Group, 2004.

Schaeffer, Francis. *How Should We Then Live?* Fleming Revell, 1976.

Silvoso, Ed. *Ekklesia*. Chosen Books, 2017.

Smith, Steven D. *Pagans & Christians in the City*. Eerdmans, 2011.

Soerens, Matthew and Hwang, Jenny. *Welcoming the Stranger*. InterVarsity Press, 2009.

Stark, Rodney. *The Triumph of Christianity*. Harper One, 2012.

Stetzer, Ed. *Subversive Kingdom*. B&H Publishing Group, 2012.

Teetsel, Eric. "Religious Freedom in 10 Minutes." Patheos.com.

Wallnau, Lance. *God's Chaos Candidate*. Killer Sheep Media, Inc., 2016.

# · ABOUT THE AUTHOR ·

Dr. John Jackson is a dynamic and strategic leader who has demonstrated organizational leadership skills in his work with national and global organizations and ministries. He has written and authored nine books on leadership, cultural change, and spiritual formation and is a sought after speaker and executive consultant.

Currently serving as the sixth president of William Jessup University, Dr. Jackson has overseen the growth of the university to more than triple in enrollment, and increased its budget from $17 million in 2011 to over $65 million in 2020. The university has been named the third-fastest growing institution of its type in the nation and is listed as the highest ranked regional college in California, and #1 for Social Mobility. Prior to joining Jessup, John served as the co-founder/CEO of Thriving Churches International and in the Office of the Senior Pastor of Bayside Church, Granite Bay, CA. He was the founding pastor at LifePoint Church in Minden, Nevada, and executive minister of the American Baptist Churches of the Pacific Southwest (now Transformation Ministries), where he served more than 270 churches in four western states. John also served as a senior and staff pastor in Oxnard and Buena Park, CA.

Dr. Jackson holds a Ph.D. and an M.A. in Educational Administration and Organizational Studies from the University of California, Santa Barbara; an M.A. in Theology (Christian Formation and Discipleship) from Fuller Theological Seminary; and a B.A. in Religion (Christian History and Thought) from Chapman University. He lives, works, and writes from Rocklin, CA, with his wife Pamela. Together they have five grown children, three sons-in love, three grandchildren, and a dog named Max.

For more information about Dr. Jackson and WJU, visit drjohnjackson.com and jessup.edu.

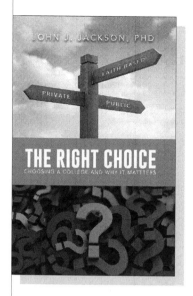

# The Right Choice: Choosing a College and Why It Matters

BY JOHN JACKSON

Choosing a college is one of life's biggest decisions, perhaps second only to marriage in human terms. How do you make the right choice? This little book has a big impact on readers grappling with their dreams, desires, and details. Dr. Jackson is a college president, pastor, and parent of five children.

He has walked hundreds of families through this decision matrix and provides helpful tips for students, family members, and friends who will take this journey together. *The Right Choice* gives you data, decision points, and a framework for shaping this decision as well as a host of other "right choices."

# Pastorpreneur: Creative Ideas for Birthing Spiritual Life in Your Community

BY JOHN JACKSON

A Christianity Today survey identified the most common self-described leadership weaknesses to be in strategizing, visioning, and entrepreneurial skills. But there is a tension that exists between dreaming, vision-casting, and being able to actually pull it off.

What is from God, what is from our own imaginations, how do we recognize the difference, and then what do we do with it?

In *Pastorpreneur*, pastor and speaker John Jackson equips pastors to employ businesslike strategic planning and innovation skills to enhance their congregational leadership. Jackson's practical strategies and grand vision will empower you to explore new methods for maximum impact on your church and community and become the church that you and God dreamed of.

# Finding Your Place In God's Plan: Forty Ways to Get There

BY JOHN JACKSON

Uncover your unique spiritual gifts to discover the special role you play in God's plan. By focusing on your passion, gifts, and personal style, Dr. John Jackson will help you explore how your unique set of spiritual gifts makes you perfect for serving God and the world. *Finding Your Place in God's Plan* is a forty-day journey... complete with daily devotionals and small group materials. Perfect for church and small group use as well.

You will be immersed in a journey of self-discovery, discerning not only your gifts and how to use them, but also the significance of those gifts for God's plan. This book contains teaching, daily devotionals, and small group materials. Successfully used in a number of churches, this book is great for a church campaign.

John Jackson & Lorraine Bossè-Smith

# LEVERAGING
### YOUR LEADERSHIP STYLE

Maximize Your Influence
by Discovering the Leader Within

STUDY GUIDE INCLUDED

# Leveraging Your Leadership Style: Maximize Your Influence by Discovering the Leader Within

BY JOHN JACKSON
AND LORRAIN BOSSÈ-SMITH

Want to awaken the hidden leader within? Ready to increase your influence and become the leader you were intended to be? *Leveraging Your Leadership Style* takes the guesswork out of the equation and offers concrete solutions to obtain greater results and success. This is not your typical leadership book.

Discover your unique leadership style in this dynamic, fast, yet informative book. Maximize your strengths and become more effective in whatever you do, no matter what the role. Seize this opportunity to transform your leadership style and take people where they might never dare to go when left to their own devices! A complete study guide is included so that you can study in groups.